OPTIONS

OPTIONS

Approaches for the Religious Education of Adolescents

PIERRE BABIN

Translated and Adapted by
John F. Murphy

HERDER AND HERDER

1967
HERDER AND HERDER NEW YORK
232 Madison Avenue, New York 10016

Original edition: *Options,*
Lyons, Editions du Chalet, 1965.

Nihil obstat: Leo J. Steady, Censor Librorum
Imprimatur: ✠ Robert F. Joyce, Bishop of Burlington
December 21, 1966

Library of Congress Catalog Card Number: 67–14140
© 1967 by Herder and Herder, Inc.
Manufactured in the United States of America

CONTENTS

PART TWO: RELIGIOUS EDUCATION
Preparation for Today's World

PREFACE

As religion teachers in the formal structure of a Catholic high school, or as CCD teachers in an occasionally less than structured program in the parish, we are sometimes afraid to think about the effect of our teaching. We place the emphasis on the student's side: how he should react, why he doesn't, the influence of the home, the parish, the former training. Occasionally, we look at ourselves and admit that we are not adequately trained; but we don't always look at ourselves and say that we are essentially responsible for the presence of God in our students at this time, in this class, at this moment. I do not mean that we can be God (God Himself freely works and freely accepts obstacles to His love), but that we must assume the responsibility for a person who is present to us; we must accept the consequences of a personal encounter; we must accept the fact that God can and may become present through us.

When we accept the reality of God's acceptance of us as persons who actively share Him with our own worlds, we perhaps see our work as vital and life-giving, not as only functional. It is true that God comes to man though the sacraments and that we are preparing our students to join in a sacramental existence. Yet we are more. We too share God with our students; for the student meets God not only in a sacramental life, he meets Him in us.

Every significant human meeting affects the ones involved. We are touched by our students; they by us. Father Babin wants that touch to be truly human, revealing. He asks that it be rich, relevant, awakening. People can meet another and never become alive. This was not God's plan in meeting us.

In this book there are no simplistic approaches to meeting another. Rather there is the way of human nature, there are the ways of the present world. Man does not operate in a vacuum, nor is he always best analyzed in one. When we viewed religious education as something functional rather than personal, it was easier to accept rules and approaches and methods that prepared a person to fit into a system that seemed to work. When we now look again at the person, it is often necessary to rework the system.

This book offers insights that may provoke some comment. We are being asked to reconsider what was "sacred" to us, sacred because we felt it was untouchable, much like our image of God. As we begin to think again of the immanence of God as well as of His transcendence, perhaps we will discover that Father Babin has not removed what is essential, but has shown us how to make ourselves present once more to Him.

I have taken the liberty in preparing this translation of making some of the material more relevant to the North American scene. This does not apply to Father Babin's insights, which are applicable to adolescents on either side of the Atlantic, but to certain variations of adolescent behavior. Adolescents have universal problems expressed in local color.

St. Pius X Preparatory School   (REV.) JOHN F. MURPHY
Uniondale, New York

10

INTRODUCTION

1. A NOTE ON THE WORD "APPROACHES"

When we use the word "approaches," we are saying possibilities, some areas of exploration, that may prove profitable in our catechesis.

What are the bases for these approaches? They are the doctrinal insights, the spiritual and educational developments, that our day seems to require for an education in faith for adolescents, more especially for those in our religious-education programs of the Catholic school or the Confraternity of Christian Doctrine.

Our view is presented as a research and an interpretation; it is tied to a certain point of view, and hence a debatable one, of a world in change and of adolescence in that world.

Each age of man is unique, and yet universal. Man sees himself as the heir of earlier ages; yet he knows he must form his own ideas, his own expressions of life at his moment. It is here and now that the Holy Spirit comes to a man thinking and doing in this world.

It will be in our awareness of this age, its operations, its areas of openness, its needs, that our faith can see and prepare for the Holy Spirit. As our age moves on, our greatest challenge is to see and to be open to those areas in which the Spirit chooses to enter man. God has always spoken to man in man's needs, insights, and gifts. He does so today.

11

The approaches that follow, while not the only possible ones, will try to give an insight into the "signs of our time."

2. IS FORMAL RELIGIOUS EDUCATION STILL POSSIBLE IN THE SECOND HALF OF THE TWENTIETH CENTURY?

A need for absolute sincerity, a demanding logic, a courage which does not fear human respect, a scorn for custom and an attraction for the weak and poor and reject, an indefinable interior attraction for perfection, for an authentic Christianity, all these impel the young souls of today to a Christian boldness, to a faithfulness that is catholic, to a new and original spirituality which surprises and moves those who observe it. Is it the breath of the Spirit ("The Spirit blows where He wills," St. John says). It is a "sign of the time" which makes us rejoice that we belong to the great and difficult time that is ours and which gives us a new hope for the future.

Paul VI, Address of September 1, 1965

To proclaim Jesus Christ, to be effective witnesses to our faith, to open our students to the meaning of Christ through religious-education programs—are these still possible, workable, or even meaningfully valid in this second half of the twentieth century? Christians, teachers in the reality of their classroom situations, priests, laity, religious, are all involved in these questions.

The Council forcefully recalled to mind the fact that the Church is to be of service to the world, an instrument working for peace and unity among men. Jesus said to His disciples, "You are the salt of the earth, you are the light of the world." Yet we have not understood the meaning of the Church if we bring salvation to only some parts of the world around us, if we are the light to only certain sections of man's life and of today's world.

12

The light and the salt are not man's invention; they are of Jesus Christ. "There is salvation in no one else," says St. Peter (Acts 4, 12). We are the light when we affirm that in the faith and love of our Lord Jesus Christ is found the secret of eternal life, the source of truth, the pardon and renewal of that insoluble suffering we all bear within ourselves, even that suffering we guard ourselves against.

Now here is the crucial problem for those of us, teachers, who believe in Jesus Christ and want to open the world to the faith: we have a general, perhaps unarticulated impression that Jesus, if we dare to speak with the realism of the Eucharist, is no longer food or drink to today's man, and perhaps will not be either to the man of the future.

Youth today are going to take possession of the earth as never before. It is the world that counts. As for Jesus Christ, John Lennon of the Beatles was correct in his observation that His popularity is on the wane. In *The Times* of London, after the second session of the Council, it was said that the Church was a venerable institution which came to life a hundred years too late, so what has the world to expect from such sluggard discussion?

Speak of grace to some students today and they yawn. Talk about heaven and hell and they listen with a mixture of interest and skepticism. Announce to them Christ the Saviour, Christ the Truth who speaks to the world, and we wonder if we should continue to teach.

What have we to say to the world that is vital, valuable, enlightening? What have we to say to the people of South America, Asia, Africa, to the newly emerging nations, to the hungry, poor, underdeveloped peoples of the world? What do we say to the space scientist, the industrialist, the worker? Where are the words

13

of Jesus which formerly gave life to the hope of the common man?

With the young American or European who no longer believes in human values, should we temporarily forget about speaking of a certain person who was crucified, who transcended human history? Will it be necessary, for a time at least, to forego religious education which no longer works for an education which is more concerned about the world and implicitly about man? For such students, tired with religion and disgusted with the teaching of it, will it be necessary to stop formal instruction for a time? Must we stop giving the good news?

To these problems with which many teachers of the faith are concerned, these approaches want to offer an answer, not in a definitive and absolute manner, but more in the way of insight and suggestion. The teacher himself will have to answer the decisive question: How to make religious instruction relevant in our day, how to see catechetics in terms of man's needs and desires expressed in the areas of freedom, action, efficiency, human values, social problems, international dimensions, all the signs of our time that call out to man and represent him today.

Above all else, can we keep our fingers on the pulse of our world? The changes which are affecting our world are still in rapid motion. For the first time in history, civilization is no longer defined in terms of faithfulness to the past and to cultural heritages passed on by previous generations, but is now considered in terms of what will come. Humanity looks only forward, so that today it is demanded of religion teachers that they move with the world, continually rethink, adapt, invent, and finally accept the movement and change of the world. Such seems to be the fundamental dimension for action and for a life-giving apostolate.

What is characteristic of the adolescent generation today is that it must move into a world that is in unceasing motion and change. The notion that adolescence is best seen in relation to its growth towards the adult world of stability is no longer tenable. While it is true that adolescence is a time of passage and growth, the adult world to which the adolsecent is heading no longer has the stability of earlier generations. As a result, the adolescent needs today not a teacher of traditional wisdom, but an educator of change and adaptability. And the first thing the students want to find in a teacher is the ability to look at the world today, to adjust to the movements in the world. With this attitude and approach, he will mean something to these students who are looking for truth.

So these approaches to a growth in Christ are not intended to give ready-made solutions. In presenting questions and provoking thought, in always being conscious of the movement of history, they will perhaps awaken the spirit, give impetus to research and reflection on the signs of our time; they will, perhaps, stimulate a constant rethinking and meeting in our minds of the encounter of the present and the eternal.

The change today, the urgency of the change in our lives and our thinking, —this is the challenge of the world. Is it not also our chance, our opportunity? It is a chance not only to possess the faith as a permanent property, but more to receive it each hour, each day, as a gift of God. It is the question of not being able to give the faith unless we have first rediscovered it truly alive in the world, in the love of man, and in the obedience to the Church, the Church alive to the present time.

15

PART ONE

RELIGIOUS EDUCATION

Good News for the Twentieth Century

I.

THE KINGDOM

Religious education must present the realities of the faith first and foremost as good news for the heart of man today.

1. THE IMPORTANCE OF THE GOOD NEWS

In giving direction to the education of the adolescent, this decision is perhaps the most important. If Christ remains a stranger to most of our students, is it not because the Church no longer means for them the source and the fullness of life, of goodness, of freedom that Jesus Christ was and is? The primary failure of our catechetical programs, apart from the deliberate free rejection of the student, seems to lie in this: revelation no longer appears as good news any more. Too frequently, the adolescent is told what he cannot do; he is told what he must learn. He is given restrictions to follow and questions to study. It is not the call to freedom, human fulfillment, salvation, a promised land, a kingdom of peace, justice, and love.

High-school students worrying about college boards, school dropouts wondering about jobs, adolescents caught up in civil-rights tensions, affluent teenagers reflecting the moods and values of our society, all of these are questioning in their own ways the meaning of life. In their own ways, they are finding a meaning of life for themselves. Will there be for them a long awaited Hope of Nations, a focal point for their lives? Unconsciously, perhaps, are they looking for Someone to call them and tell them of life, of a certainty in this world of changing values? Will this Someone reach them with words that have meaning for them and can influence them?

Will we be there for them? Are we capable of bringing to the students the story of the Messiah? Are we ready to excite them with the news of a kingdom thrust upon this world, almost two thousand years ago, by a certain Jesus of Nazareth? The whole question of catechetics today for the adolescent is, in our opinion, in this area of making our message come alive as an exciting promise of life, as the good news that Jesus gave. The approaches that follow later continue this basic idea that religious education be good news, announced as such, believed as such, and affirmed as such. The sacraments are good news. The hierarchy of the Church is part of this joyful discovery. Even the four last things, including hell, are part of the proclamation of Christ. If we do not see all these as values, as part of the new kingdom, we do not have the right to speak to our students. We become prophets of doom instead; we betray the Gospels.

The stakes are high enough to demand serious thought: let us remember what Jesus Himself did, and, in the Holy Spirit, let us try to see how we can continue His teaching in ourselves today for the adolescents with whom we are working.

When we speak about Christ's message of His kingdom, therefore, we want to characterize the style, approach, and content of His teaching, in particular during the first two years of His apostolic ministry. In Christ, the style and content, the teaching and doctrine, were one reality in a way that had never been before. Let us not, therefore, attempt to separate them.

The three major elements of the teaching of the kingdom are:

1. Christ announces a new world, a kingdom of peace, justice, and love.

2. Christ makes men experience this kingdom.

3. Christ announces this kingdom to a humanity as He found it with all its human weaknesses, imperfections, doubts.

1. Christ Directs Men's Thought to a Kingdom of Peace, Justice, and Love

When Christ appears, He begins by announcing the greatest happiness possible. He does not speak of death, but of life; not of penance first, but of His kingdom. Of course, Jesus calls men to penance and invites them to carry His cross, but this happens only later. We are called to penance and the cross because of what He offers. It is all directed to the kingdom. He says, "The time is fulfilled, and the kingdom of God is at hand; repent and believe in the Gospel" (Mk. 1, 15). Yet His first words are "the kingdom of God is at hand."

The beatitudes tell us the conditions for entry into the kingdom. Yet we sometimes forget which part comes first. It is not "the poor" but rather "Blessed are they . . ."

At last here was someone who could say His message is good news. The poor could rejoice, the blind, the oppressed, all those overcome by the burdens of life. There was not one of His words that did not announce joy and abundance; even His warnings,

His reproaches, His curses were in relation to His good news. He brought man life and an abundance of life. His passion and His death were to be but a road to life; and, if the Father pruned His vine, it was in order that it might "bear more fruit."

Let no one be confused. If Jesus speaks of His kingdom, of the resurrection and life, it is not only as a device to get the attention of His hearers. He knows the kingdom; He experiences it Himself; and, if we dare say it, He feels Himself at every moment of His existence as abundance, life, eternity, in the midst of men.

He is salvation "in flesh and blood"; He is salvation become man. And because He knows this, His message of His kingdom takes on an urgency drawing us on. His message touches on our deepest yearnings and desires for fulfillment. In Jesus Christ there is a personal awareness of the happiness He offers us, of the kingdom He invites us to.

It is impossible here to describe fully this theme of the kingdom, but we can measure its implications for our catechetical approach. Before we concern ourselves with the instructional problem, however, let us ask ourselves this question: Are we really convinced that in Jesus Christ and in His name we are the messengers and witnesses of Christ, for all men coming into this world, that we are the bearers of a message which is fundamentally life-giving and beneficial for the whole world?

You can hear educators saying, "Don't speak of Christ, of faith. This bores our students." Yet has not the real problem been missed? The idea is not merely to talk about a certain Jesus Christ; rather, it is to make Christ present, the Christ who is this new kingdom, who is life-giving and who offers all this to us. We have no more than that to do, and our hearers will not turn away in boredom, unless our message is blocked by sin or by our own lifeless manner of bringing it to our classes. If, in effect, we speak only to give more or less boring words on religion, we should remain silent, for we are betraying Christ.

Effect of the kingdom teaching on our approach:
Our religious instruction must be that of good news.

We can now formulate the first law of religious education, one which comes before all else, for it is deeply rooted in the very heart of Christ's message: Our teaching must be good news for the man of today.

First of all, it must be good news for us who are the teachers. This brings us to the first question bearing on this topic: Have we ourselves grasped the message, the entire message, as good news? Do we live the faith as an extraordinary gift to ourselves, a source of new light and life in ourselves?

It seems that, if the teachers of youth are having trouble getting the message of Christ across to their students, the problem is here: teachers are not conscious enough of being bearers of this great gift of good news; they have not discovered for themselves the reality of this good news. They know but they do not experience it.

The good news is for our classes. It is not enough that the message of Christ be understood by us only. It must be presented as such and received as such by the adolescents with whom we work. And this brings us to another point, dealing with the problem of reaching the adolescent mind.

Before analyzing the intellectual elements of a dogmatic truth,

before presenting an abstract definition or a moral law, it is necessary to present the revealed truth as good news which can reach
and can appeal to the students.

Let us take for an example an extremely difficult, almost paradoxical truth, hell, for it is a complex doctrinal point in terms of
the idea of good news.

How do you describe hell as a sign of the good news? Or more
precisely, how do you present the total teaching of revelation on
this topic as good news?

To answer this problem in catechetics, we must first of all ask
ourselves what is the reality of hell and all that the teaching on it
implies. Does it mean to us a truth and an insight into the glory
and grandeur of God and of man? In the second place, we must
look for the best manner of giving this truth to our students today, in such a way that they understand effectively the possibility
of hell as a gift of God and one of the aspects of His love for man.
For we must consider ourselves that God's love is such that He, in
order to assure man of the measure of man's own greatness, has
taken the enormous risk of allowing from man a definitive refusal of His love.

We can see clearly in this example of hell that the problem for
the religion teacher is twofold:

1. The teacher must understand the complete doctrinal reality
of hell in its fullness. It must be understood, on the one hand, that
hell represents the last resort of a clear human freedom which sets
itself up in opposition to all community and is determined to exist
only for itself. On the other hand, in spite of his absolute refusal
to join with others in community, the person damned to hell is in
the realm of God's love and infinite mercy, although not sharing

24

in it. (It must be pointed out that God does not hate anyone. It is the freedom of the person that cuts the individual off from God's love.)

Thus understood, and although the dimensions of the love of God remain a mystery for us, hell becomes a witness to the infinite respect of God for man's freedom. We can say, perhaps, that the doctrine of hell shows this respect of God for man more clearly than any other doctrine. Beyond these considerations, if hell appears absurd and monstrous to ourselves and our students, is it not because we have not thought out the full implications of the doctrine on hell?

2. The second problem is one of teaching. It is here a question of breaking through the barriers that students face in front of the idea of hell as good news, and then helping them to open to this idea through their own experiences of freedom which will help them to see the mystery of faith.

Thus we would be able to help them understand what hell is for one who goes there, not through stupidity or thoughtlessness, but who goes to hell because of a free choice. It is a dismal choice, perhaps, but a definitive choice, a choice of sin.

We should help the student understand that if a person remains in hell, it is not in spite of his efforts to escape, but rather it is through his eternal and radical and free choice to reject all forms of union with others.

It is important, moreover, to present hell, as much as one can speak of it, in a more purified image than the one given to our parents. To the student generation, very open to human relations, we can present hell as the place where people take themselves too seriously, so seriously that a person becomes immersed within himself, refusing all communication with anyone outside himself. By definition, the damned is one who is in hell because he is incapable of dialogue, incapable because he refuses to open to another, because he refuses any exchange, any acceptance of himself with others. It will be up to the teacher, to be sure, to find the words and the images that will open for the students the truth about hell.

2. Christ Makes Men Experience the Kingdom

Christ was not content just to speak of the kingdom; He makes men experience it, in His person, in His actions, in His very way of speaking.

Do we remember the reasons put forth at the first attempt to arrest Jesus? "He seduces the crowd." The rulers and the Pharisees sent attendants to seize Him, but the men sent to take Jesus justified and excused themselves for not arresting Him by saying to the Pharisees, "No man ever spoke like this man!" The Pharisees retorted to the men, "Are you led astray, you also?" (Jn. 7, 47). He seduced the crowds and "the crowds were astonished at his teaching" (Mt. 7, 28).

In our own time when we have become very conscious of the respect due the individual person, when we are aware of interpersonal relationships, when we are conscious of the danger to the person by pressures from hidden persuaders, when we are helped by a greater maturity of conscience,[1] the word "seducer" and all it implies sounds strange to us. Jesus—a seducer? Yes, but not in the sense the Pharisees wished to have their hearers understand it —that Christ abused the people. In that context we would have to say that Christ had violated the individual's freedom by His appeals to their collective unconscious, to their unfulfilled desires. This would be contrary to the care which was His for individual freedom and to which the Gospel bears witness. He called, not for an unconscious response, not for a mob response based on an emotional appeal, but for a most personal choice.

But we must admit that Jesus presented Himself to the crowds following Him as an extraordinarily fascinating person who appealed to the sense of liberty and conscience. He was a marvelous speaker, full of authority. He was a worker of miracles in the eyes of Herod. He was a leader of men: "Come, follow me . . ."— "We have found the Messiah."—"They left all and followed Him." He was a truly alive person, so that we could say He was one who lived life to its fullest. He was a fascinating person. "Happy the mother who gave birth to such a son." An encounter with Him brought life again to Mary Magdalene and the Samaritan woman.

If Jesus multiplied miracles, however, if the blind saw, if the deaf heard, if the lame walked, it was not so much to furnish apologetical arguments to prove the divine origin of the Church He would establish, but to make known, to make visible and appealing the beginning of the messianic age, the days of joy and

1. We are speaking here of the concept of maturity of conscience as it has been developed mainly by Freud and Rogers.

renewal, the days of fulfillment that had been promised and announced by the prophets.

It is significant that the synoptic writers, faithful witnesses of the teachings of Christ, insist on the close link between Jesus' announcement of the kingdom and the healings He performed everywhere He went. "And he went about all Galilee, teaching in their synagogues and preaching the gospel of the kingdom and healing every disease and every infirmity among the people" (Mt. 4, 23).

The Lord did not do any differently with the group of disciples. Before anything else, He gave them the chance to discover how good it felt to be together with Him, to live a life of sons of God, to know a certain quality of spiritual freedom. "He took them aside." He united them as a group, had them live a common life. He made them enter into His divine friendship, had them taste it before revealing to them its fullness and its demands. And if one tries to find out what brought them back together on that first day of the week after they fled from the crucifixion (and before they knew of the resurrection), it becomes almost evident that it was because they had had the unique experience of three years lived in the intimacy of the Master.

And finally, we cannot ignore the catechetical style, the teaching of Jesus, His way of speaking to the people. He does not try to explain, but He announces. He does not begin by defining, but by having hearers respond and taste, by stirring in His audiences infinite desires. Can we find in the entire Gospel one precise and definitive statement of the kingdom of God? No, but on the other hand we find many parables which open up a world which men would never have dreamt about. When they asked Him why His disciples did not fast, Jesus answered, "Can the wedding guests mourn as long as the bridegroom is with them?" The parables and messages of Christ would have been those of a fanatic if they had not been sanctioned by "signs," by undeniable facts, in particular by the sign of the resurrection.

Jesus did not address Himself to man's reason alone. He spoke to the whole man, the senses, the mind, the imagination, the heart, the intelligence. He did it by His way of being and speaking, His manner of living and acting. He identified with the people; He appealed to their enthusiasms. Yet He went even farther. He made the people experience the kingdom in many ways.

For ourselves we are not to copy slavishly His style or His words. What is necessary for our teaching today is that we have His spirit which He communicates to us and through which we can communicate His teaching to the world today.

Implication for our teaching:
Our religious instruction must help adolescents experience the kingdom.

We now have the second factor to consider in teaching adolescents: When we are teaching the faith, it is absolutely necessary that our students experience the faith as a kingdom, a promised land, as salvation for themselves today.

The Christian community is the place for such an experience of the kingdom. It is in this community that the adolescent can be freed from the fascination of the limited world around him and opened to the richness and fullness of the knowledge and life which Jesus Christ is and which He will share with the student.

In this community the student is called to experience the reality of the good news; in it he should come to know the power of the resurrection as an actual event lived by the Church, the people of God.

This experience of the kingdom can be brought about in many ways. It may be on a retreat, a day of recollection, during a Mass in which the adolescent becomes truly involved, truly feels that he is co-celebrating. It may be during a group discussion that he suddenly comes to see a point, discovers that the good news is not just a moral program which "tomorrow" (in his adult days) he will have to think seriously about, but a message directed to him here and now. Especially during his impressionistic age can he experience the kingdom in knowing and experiencing friendship with a person in whom Christ lives. It may come from serving others, perhaps in an organized, school-year-long program of assistance to the poor, the blind, the outcasts of the neighborhood.

The teacher should be a man in whom Christ lives, a man who, in his relationship with his students, will help them experience the kingdom. It is in the teacher that adolescents should come to realize the truth of the resurrection, that Jesus Christ lives in each of them and calls each of them to His kingdom. And whether the students will experience this call, this kingdom, depends on whether they experience, as it were, their teacher. Thus it is that we teachers must witness to and live the kingdom, not only in what we teach, but in the way we teach; the atmosphere which we give to and encourage in our class is as important as what is taught. One thing is certain: the good news cannot be "taught," in the sense of systematizing it and presenting it in a purely didactic or analytical way; if this is done, then our students learn

30

perhaps about the faith, but they do not come to live it. The letter abides always, but the spirit prevails. "I am the door; if any one enters by me, he will be saved, and will go in and out and find pasture. . . . I came that they may have life, and have it abundantly" (Jn. 10, 9. 10).

3. Christ Announces the Kingdom to Sinners

We have now come to the last aspect of the teaching of the kingdom, namely, that Jesus approached not perfect men, but imperfect men; He invited to the kingdom those who doubt, those who lack perseverance, the prodigals. He placed his teaching in the very heart of human reality, a reality which sometimes seemed contrary to and most unlike the reality of the kingdom of heaven.

What would seem more unlikely in the eyes of men, even in the eyes of the apostles, than the fact that Jesus was willing to talk with the Samaritan woman, with Mary Magdalene? Yet it was in such meetings, such dialogues, that He revealed who He was: the Messiah, and what that meant: salvation.

What could be more unlikely than to reveal to the men He met and talked with that they were the sons of God, and then to invite them to their Father's kingdom? If Jesus had been content to announce to men a certain participation, more or less abstract, in the divine life, He would not have been killed for it. But to have announced this kingdom to and for the poor, to bring the Gospel to the blind, the deaf, the outcast, was to contradict the established ideas of the messianic kingdom to come. Jesus dared to take His message into the troubled and very violent human and political hopes of the messianic visions of the Jewish nation.

Also, have we understood how unlikely or how unexpectedly human were the comparisons which the Lord used in order to give His hearers an idea of what the kingdom was like? He chose images rich in human experience: the pearl beyond price, the great banquet, the wedding feast. These images, full of the human, full of life, were, supposedly, so unlike the kingdom of heaven.

It is evidently not a question of saying here that Jesus is attempting to confuse His hearers with natural images of His supernatural kingdom, or trying to obscure His teaching, of being deliberately ambiguous about His teaching. He is not so in His person, nor in His words, nor in His attitude. We understand that Jesus does not fear to start from human realities when He teaches, even if the human realities are marked by sin and are part of the human experience. The human realities are confusing and contradictory. He announces the good news to come within the framework of the human condition; and, at the same time, by His own being, by His presence, by His words, He purifies and frees us of the weaknesses of the human condition. The human condition, in Him and through Him, is a reality wherein we can discover and unearth the power of salvation, of revelation, of the good news. So, at the beginning of His work, Jesus did not hesitate to risk some confusion by His use of human terms and hopes in announcing to us the good news to come in the theme of a kingdom. The apostles, even in the days after the resurrection, still did not understand the full meaning of Christ's life. They wanted to know if He was going to restore the kingdom of Israel. At one point Christ had to restrain the crowds lest they make Him a king. He announced that His kingdom was not of this

32

world. It would take His entire life, death, resurrection, and ascension to make His people understand. Only then would their confused human hopes, ideas, aspirations become purified by His teaching. Yet it is through their human hopes, ideas, and aspirations that He brings them to the new kingdom.

Implications for our teaching:
Our teaching of the message of Christ must be announced to our students as we discover them with their weaknesses, imperfections, and doubts.

One final note: The teacher, under the influence, often charismatic, of the Holy Spirit, and in fidelity to the tradition and teachings of the Church, will never hesitate in his language and style of teaching to open up to his students the revelation of Christ in terms of the human condition, in terms of man's weaknesses, his emotional and intellectual confusion, the contradictions in his nature, "the evil that is in him."

Perhaps one is tempted to remark, "But Jesus was God. He could do things which we should never dare to do. He knew His hearers better than we know our students." Of course, this observation is true, insofar as it means that we should never dare to take chances in our teaching, challenge our students beyond their capacity, confuse them with a paradox before they are able to perceive its paradoxical quality, and so forth. Yet we should not fear to reveal life. Our teaching should not operate in a vacuum, life going on all around but never in the classroom, having to do with everything else about our students except their faith. Did not the Church in Council courageously dare to rediscover the sources of her life in the world, and to engage in honest dialogue with the world? We might very well avoid deviating from "true doctrine" in our teaching if we are purely intellectual in our approach, purely formal, if we refuse to take into account the actual human situation when we teach our students. But in so doing, we have less chance, and perhaps no chance, of giving them the good news of the kingdom. We will tell them about the kingdom, but never get around to inviting them to it.

In the past we have perhaps forgotten, because of some Jansenist spirit still alive in our time, that the whole man, flesh and spirit, is invited to the kingdom of God. Dare we, who speak of salvation history, forget that the flesh, man's instincts, were created and willed by God, as providential gifts for spiritual growth, as means for gaining spiritual truth? Do we unconsciously regard man's pleasure in earthly goods as a kind of necessary evil, activity below religious par, an embarrassment to Christianity? Are we not unconsciously of the mind that a certain part of creation is there only to tempt us? Have we forgotten the place of the human in the work of grace and salvation?

The instincts, for example, play a major part in the psychological and spiritual formation of man, especially of the adolescent, as Oraison has suggested: "The period of adolescence is the last stage of instinctive rising above a barrier in this sense, that the adolescent must, in order to adapt himself to the life that will soon be his, relinquish a certain infantile security in which he is at ease because of his restricted circumstances. The unfolding of impulses in an adult key urges him on almost in spite of himself. His great hardship consists in taking on this blossoming process harmoniously so as to enter on adult or oblative behavior, as Freud would say, in a positive way. The adolescent often reacts

34

to this interior impulse which baffles him and shatters his whole equilibrium by stiffening his defenses: processes such as moral response, ascesis, thirst for the Absolute."[2]

Let us rejoice, therefore, in the abundance of sources of life in our nature, and reflect on their good uses, not about how to stifle them. Stifling of the good and natural instincts in an adolescent, as Oraison goes on to say, often leads to a great frustration, "excessive and hypersensitive idealism," an unreal world, heading towards an unreal kingdom.

Evidently, if one dares to touch human nature as it is, to live from the life his students are experiencing in a profound communion with all that is human, he will not have a tranquil time of it. Thus the Christian teacher, in taking prudent chances with the teaching of the kingdom, must not cease to implore the Holy Spirit for assistance in order to remain faithful to the word of God. He will unceasingly refer to others more expert than himself for guidance and knowledge so as to maintain and improve his perspective of the human. He will remember that the flesh is weak, and can weaken the spirit. He knows that although the Counsellor is in each of his students, guiding him, the devil is there outside trying to lead him astray.

But he is aware, too, that his students want to live in a Church, to be a part of a Church that is not afraid, that lives and believes in—and affirms human progress and human life. He will have this principle to go by: Prudence is not fear, but intelligence in the service of love, clear thinking in the service of generous giving.

2. In "Some Light from Depth Psychology on Adolescence," in *Modern Catechetics,* edited by Gerard S. Sloyan, New York, 1963, p. 353.

2. THE NECESSITY OF TEACHING
THE GOOD NEWS

(Why This Insistence on the Teaching of the Kingdom?)

1. The Teaching of the Kingdom:
A Message Especially Relevant to Our Day

Has what so many teachers of religion have done in the past, often in a rigorously systematic and analytical manner, suddenly become valueless and radically unsuitable to the teaching of Jesus Christ?

Needless to say, the answer is yes. Yet there is no need to spend our time criticizing the ways of the past, except insofar as they persist today to the disadvantage of religious education. Rather, our concern must be today's world, today's troubles, this generation's dreams and failures. And today has often been called the post-Christian era. It is post-Christian because it has forgotten the good news, because Christianity is no longer a shaping influence on world development, because men of today no longer hear the call to the heavenly kingdom. In a sense, therefore, it is post-Christian but also pre-Christian; and this means that the world must be *evangelized*. For as the *Pastoral Constitution on the Church in the Modern World* says, "the Church knows that her message is in harmony with the most secret desires of the human heart . . . Far from diminishing man, her message brings to his development light, life, and freedom. Apart from this message nothing will avail to fill up the heart of man: 'Thou hast made us

36

for thyself,' O Lord, 'and our hearts are restless until they rest in thee' " (Article 21).

Now an evangelization supposes and requires, as a fundamental basis, the teaching of the kingdom. Why?

By definition, to evangelize is to say, to make present the good news. And how do we say the good news if we do not present it to the heart of man, the man who is searching for the good in life? How can the good news be announced if we do not reach man in his very own desires, in the images which fill up his dreams, in his everyday life of joy or despair? How can we spread the good news, if the men we are addressing hear only words describing some unreal event, some far-away time? How can we evangelize if our hearers do not experience in some way the ever-present resurrection, if they do not discover the presence of God at the very heart of their own life?

2. The Teaching of the Kingdom: A Message Especially Relevant to the Adolescent

There is a kind of parallelism between the situation of our world, considered as a particular historical period, and the particular time of adolescence. They, both the twentieth-century world and its adolescents, are discovering the invigoration of liberty, the extraordinary possibilities of man, the ambition to create and become, the sense of progress, the excitement of living on this earth. One could even say that the characteristics of adolescense are only adding to those characteristics of our times. Both have the same profound need, both make the same cry: Where is the Messiah?

The world of today and the adolescent are both forced to choose a new world. Yet these worlds need evangelization more than anything else because they are issuing from a stable situation of Christendom, and yet do not know to which god to entrust their futures; all values must be thought anew because of the changes in mental structures and ways of living brought about by changes in science and technology in the one world and the changes in body and mind in the adolescent. The extraordinary success of the book *Honest to God* is a perceptive sign of our time: we are doing away with an image of God, of religion, of life. But for what?

The adolescent is caught between two worlds. The world of childhood is slowly disappearing from under him, that solid and faultless world where he had voluntarily accepted his parents' outlook on the world. The adult world is now opening up; it is an unknown, undiscovered world, strange and fascinating all at once, where he will be able to enter as a Christian only after he personally and vitally assumes the faith and way of life his parents had formerly given him.

Between the two certain worlds, childhood and adult, the alolescent's heart, his yearnings, his instincts, his intelligence, are full of starts and hesitations. In the liveliness of his new life vital questions arise: How will he make out in life? Whom can he turn to for answers? What values will he give to his life? He is searching for something to live for, something to die for.

This very new situation in regard to childhood calls for a renewed presentation of the Christian message. It is the same for the world around us today also as it breaks out of its old way of doing and believing. Of course, it is not a question of doing away with the religious formation received during childhood, or doing away with the forms received from the Christian tradition in the past centuries of the world. But to a new world, to a new problem, must go a new answer. We must once more go out and sow; we must once more give a new presentation of the Gospel message, speak it in a way that will appeal to the heart of man today. Is this not the way of the Spirit, the meaning of the Council, the purpose of the Church's astonishing, scarcely begun *aggiornamento?*[3]

There is another reason why the world and especially today's youth need to be evangelized, need to hear the call of the kingdom: the ascendancy of what might be called the "pagan kingdom," a substitute kingdom made up of man's marvelous technological successes and their results—greater material comfort, greater wealth, almost total supervision of earthly destiny; but made up also of a number of unfortunate side-effects of technological society: life in what Harvey Cox has described as "the giant switchboard" or the "cloverleaf," life being characterized by constant, enervating communication and motion. It is an age

3. Karl Rahner asks, "Can it be maintained that the Church has consummated her *aggiornamento,* that she has fulfilled the task given her? Can we say that the Church is now youthful and fresh, eager to confront the unknown spiritual adventures lying in the future for a mankind of so great number, a mankind which is highly organized, technologically sophisticated, automated, capable of influencing its own future development, of reaching out to the super-terrestrial realms of outer space which portend so much good and so much deadly terror? It would certainly not be advisable, and in fact one should dare not attempt, to make such a claim. Nothing would be more dangerous than an over-enthusiastic attitude. The Council marked the decisive beginning of the *aggiornamento,* it established the renewal, it called us to the ever necessary repentance and return; in other words, it was only the beginning of the beginning." From *The Church After the Council* (New York and London, 1966), pp. 19–20.

which has little time for reflection, little reverence for or remembrance of past values. In the face of this rising up of the "gods that are in the blood," do we not feel the urgency to deepen human experience for our students, to reveal the fundamental and wonderful meaning of human life as revealed in and by Jesus Christ? We must struggle not to let the varieties of profane experience nullify the life-giving religious experience of our students.[4]

3. CONCLUSION

Nothing is more important for the adolescent than the experience of the meaning of the kingdom of Christ.

Some years ago there appeared an important novel for understanding the adolescent, *The Wanderer,* by Alain-Fournier.[5] Perhaps it was an important novel for the adolescents themselves, precisely because it hit upon one of the key elements in the adolescent soul: the search and discovery of a "paradise" that signified the adult world they wanted. Alain-Fournier put these significant words on the lips of his hero, an adolescent fed up with his routine existence, whose wanderings bring him one night in the midst of a feast at the castle of his dreams: "A man who has once leaped into paradise, how could he put up afterwards with ordinary life?"

An adolescent, a youth, is essentially someone in search of be-

4. In the prayer for the Fourth Sunday after Easter, we pray: "O God, in whom all the faithful are united in one mind, let your people everywhere love your commandments and yearn for what you promise, so that, even amid the changes of this world, their hearts may always be fixed upon true happiness."

5. *The Wanderer* is available in a Doubleday Anchor Book edition.

coming, of discovering fullness in life, of finding success. It is someone who is spontaneously convinced that he will succeed, even if this is in contrast with his parents' view and with the adult world he finds around him. Now from an educational view, what is most important is that, in his search, he should make a leap into the real "paradise." One encounter may not seem much, but it can be decisive and it cannot be forgotten.

Adolescence is not meant to be a time of mature religious experience, an occasion for complete spiritual fulfillment; but it is a time and an occasion to create an appeal to the adolescent's heart, to have him sense, to discover, and then to start on a never-ending search to find what he has sensed. It is to keep going higher, to surpass himself in grasping again and again what was once glimpsed in a moment of meaning, in an experience of the kingdom. Such is adolescence in its greatest moment.

We should realize that it is extremely important that this experience of the kingdom, this leap into paradise, not be a false one, a somewhat deceptive experience of a make-believe world. What a crime when the supposed entrance into the kingdom is nothing more than a dull meeting with fellow students on a Sunday. On the other hand, what a disappointment for later on in life if this "leap into paradise" is based on some pious actions without any basis in the real world of the adolescent. On the contrary, what a fullness of life is realized if the introduction to the kingdom is made in such a way that the student feels he has come into a true "paradise." It may be a paradise marked by friendship, unselfishness, a new free life with Jesus Christ. This youth will be marked for life, whatever his life may be. He will never forget and will look for the experience again and again.

This discovery may happen in an instant, or it may develop over many years. It may occur on the occasion of a talk, a retreat, a day of recollection, a time of working for others. When it occurs is a secret of God.

The important thing is this: The teacher should direct all things to assure that this discovery may happen. The teacher has been sent to the adolescent to say to his students as Jesus said to him: The kingdom is here. Come and see.

4. REFLECTIONS

1. *A message that is good news.*

a. Before presenting the message, have I discovered in what way it is good news for me?

b. Am I preoccupied with presenting a message as good news for the heart of the adolescent today, a message which reaches his thinking and actual reactions?

2. *A message which announces the kingdom.*

a. Am I a sign, a witness, of the kingdom by my own life and thought?

b. Does my thinking, my acting, express for our own days the message of the Risen Christ?

c. Does my teaching, my speaking, announce the kingdom? Does this message of Christ reach the adolescent in his own needs, his activities, his life?

3. *A message that leads the adolescent to experience the kingdom.*

a. Am I interested in those actual experiences of the adolescent that can lead him to an experience of the kingdom, that is, friendships, outings, dates, parties?

b. Am I attentive to the quality of the life within a group, the interpersonal relationships, the potential for the growth of an individual, the effect of shared experiences?

4. *A message which unfolds revelation to the person as he is.*

a. Do I show my love for man and the world in the name and manner of Jesus Christ?

b. Does my style, my language, keep up with the life around me? Do I find it important to use all the realities of the world in my evangelization? Do I see the role of all creation in our lives so that all of creation may become a source of grace and salvation?

II.

HUMAN VALUES

Today an open concern for understanding and developing all the dimensions of man is a grace, a gift of God. In an awareness of the meaning of revelation for today, and in the spirit of the Gospel, catechists will strive to educate the adolescent to a new style, perhaps best called a contemporary style of the Christian life which is relevant to the world. It will be a renewed expression for our time of the Christian life, one that is faithful to the human values that the world is concerned with.

1. THE SIGNIFICANCE OF THIS APPROACH

In the above stated approach, two factors are important:

1. A new style, a contemporary approach to the Christian life, which is relevant to today's world.

2. An approach to the Christian life which is faithful to human values.

This approach, then, is not exclusively concerned with teaching only. It is not directed to the problem of moral and dogmatic teaching only, but more towards a search for a new approach to adolescent life today. We are searching for a new form of Christian living for youth.

1. Educating the Adolescent to a Christian Life Which Is Relevant to His World

There is no education in the faith, especially on the adolescent level, without an education towards and within the framework of his actual behavior. And, we must add, there is no education or transformation of his behavior without the witness of his teacher and the Christian community.

What is lacking most to the adolescents today is not what we could normally call "good example," but rather an example of a "new style," a form of Christian life more dynamic than static, an example of a sign correspondent to the needs and the forms of our time. The adolescents need to be a part of the movements, of the current ideas, of the problems that are being lived. They are looking and waiting for a life where the Holy Spirit shows himself in the society around them. They are, to put it bluntly, looking for a new kind of saint.

Thrown into a civilization which is in full change and upheaval, they are not satisfied by any abstract presentation of truth or by a morality not rooted in today's world. What they are asking of the teacher is a humanism, an appreciation and love of man, which permits them to become Christians and, at the same time, more a man or more a woman. They want to be fully themselves and fully Christians.[1]

From this view, the teacher of religion will have to lead his students to a new approach, a new style; and he will have to

1. See the importance of such men as Teilhard de Chardin and Dietrich Bonhoeffer, not only in their writings, but as a new type of man, having a modern outlook on the world.

help them find specific directions and moral demands relevant to the twentieth century.

2. Educating the Adolescent to a Christian Life Which Is Faithful to Human Values

What is this approach that is directed to human values? It is difficult to express it in a few words or phrases. Two lines of thought will help express it.

Human values. These are key words in our times which describe the discovery and advancement of all that is valuable in man as man. Man is the one value for our time. This focusing of attention on man goes as far as exalting all the potentials of the human person, body and soul. The youth of today want men who love life and who love the earth. All their ideas about religion revolve around the human person.

Historical progress. Everything is judged in terms of what things will be, of becoming, advancement, of marching forward. All this is done with the necessary element of optimism. We progress forward, we are inventing, we buy on credit, we put our hopes in the future. We think of all things in a regular pattern of progress. We have become very sensitive to what is possible, to what is probable. We now know that in the not too distant future it will be possible to realize certain things which are unimaginable today. We are at a time when we look on the past only to get a better grasp of the future.

In view of all this, the educator in himself and in his words will have to be such to his students that they discover in the Christian life the richness and fullness of life itself; the students will discover all the values of human life, infinitely full, passed down and saved by grace, where all the riches of revelation are lived with all the riches of this earthly life. This is the meaning of the fullness of human values. It is one of the signs of the time which we must be attuned to.

Moreover, this idea of fullness, for a Christian, cannot have its full meaning without its complementary aspect, its very condition: the cross. It is in the light of the cross, as Teilhard de Chardin suggested, that we can best understand how the divine gives the necessary dimension to our ideas of human fullness; and how the divine, in the cross, transcends our notions of human fullness. This will be the development that we will follow.

2. THE NECESSITY OF THIS APPROACH

1. Why Must We Emphasize Human Values?

The more an adolescent matures, the more he becomes the teen-ager, the more he becomes himself and prepares himself to fit into the new world around him. After the autistic phase of solitude in his development which follows after late childhood, the adolescent, having broken off with childhood, focuses his attention and his whole being towards the future. He becomes himself by building for his future, a future which will be possible only if he adopts the values esteemed by the world. Therefore, it is impossible to develop the religious personality of a student without educating him to the world of tomorrow. Of course, it may be possible, in some cases, to impose on a child the ideas and values of a previous generation;[2] but in general, this cannot be done with today's adolescent. He is much too aware of the world that is around him and the world that is going to develop.

If such is the case, we can realize the importance and the urgency of helping the young people of today to discover, in the light of the Holy Spirit, the main outlines of a twentieth-century Christian life. We must help in the development of a new form, a new style; without this the adolescents will be lost in the old forms which they will sooner or later reject. (We must say that we perhaps risk giving in to a certain fascination with changes that may make us laugh at ourselves in ten or fifteen years. Perhaps our children will laugh, in fact, with the way we have taken ourselves and the changes we want so seriously. Our concern with some changes should cease when some of them reveal themselves as having little importance in the course of history. Yet the question of change today presses against our consciences and is important in a world where our ways of thinking and feeling are overturned. We must reëvaluate, readjust, and seek the new forms for this world in which the Spirit is revealing Himself.)

"Modern societies," says Raymond Aron, "are perhaps the first in history which are not only transforming themselves, but are conscious of their transformation as an integral part of their development. Formerly, in societies of earlier times, mankind had as its ideal an established and constant social order; modern societies, however, have for their ideal an ever continuing growth and development of the social order which involves the constant restructuring of the social organizations."[3]

2. That can never be recommended, of course. But some parents can succeed in materially enclosing their children in their own universe.

3. In *Main Currents in Sociological Thought*, New York and London, 1965, p. 9.

2. Why Should We Adopt This New Approach Based on Human Values?

Our obligation stems from the fact that the adolescent is in a world in which we have a new phenomenon: the domination of man over nature. This has led men to be extremely sensitive to questions of man's productivity, expansion, development, to the areas of freedom for all men whether political, economic, or social. Chiefly, it is the great urges for social and economic development present in the world today that should impel us to direct youth to a way of life that utilizes their energies and resources in and for the world they are a part of.

In fact, if we pay attention to what can strike them the most as they enter life, we will speak of our civilization as it is:

A civilization of action which needs competent and qualified men who have acquired the necessary degrees, qualifications, social mobility, all of which are needed if a man is to produce.

A civilization of productivity whose new economic structures have created a new way of life. In yesterday's world, men tried to acquire the necessities of life, tried to save, to put aside for personal security and welfare. In today's world, nothing is put aside; money, goods, are to be placed in the ever increasing circle of exchange and production. Today we don't earn money; we make it.

A civilization of social and communitarian tendencies in which men must live and act together in order to realize the great tasks of our times and face the many changes of this world.

A civilization open to the universe in which it is no longer possible to satisfy oneself with the limited horizons of one's neigh-

49

borhood, city, or even state. Youth today travel, know different people and places, and are in direct contact with other youths with different values and beliefs.

Whether the demands of this new civilization overwhelm and frighten the adolescent, whether it fascinates and totally absorbs him, the problem is the same. We must propose an approach to the moral and spiritual life that considers the desires and demands that our new world reflects. It must be a new style, a Christianity in tune with the contemporary world.

Adolescents are more and more driven by the urge to be better than they are. The religion teacher cannot ignore these aspirations as he transmits the word of a living God, of a God who is always linked to any effort of man towards a better being. For God is Himself the source of all life; He created all things good; and, in Jesus Christ, He has revealed to us that it is the glory of the Father that we bear much fruit.

3. POSSIBLE APPROACHES

How can our religious education lead the student to an authentically Christian and authentically human existence?

We offer here three paths, three approaches, where doctrinal and educational insights come into play. These are not dogmatic statements to be followed to the letter; rather, they are suggested approaches, educational directions, possibilities for reflection. It is each teacher's responsibility to think them over and to adapt them according to the particular genius or talent given each man by the Holy Spirit.

1. A Change of Emphasis in the Presentation of the Message of Good News and a Rethinking of the Method of Transmission

The first thing we must do, it seems, is to reëxamine the presentation of the doctrine itself. Without doubt, the message will remain basically the same; but, in giving it to our students, we must attempt to have them see it in terms of the major needs of our time, to give them a new setting, a new perspective which will permit them to know these truths in the context of the modern world, and not in the context of some pre-secular netherworld.

For example, we will not have man looking towards heaven, but man looking around and concerned with the earth in the name of God.[4] We shall present the message of Christ in such

4. "In Christ we are offered the possibility of partaking in the reality of God and in the reality of the world, but not in the one without the other. The reality of God discloses itself only by setting me entirely in the reality of the world, and when I encounter the reality of the world it is always already sustained, accepted, and reconciled in the reality of God. This is the inner meaning of the revelation of God in the man Jesus Christ. . . . This does not mean that 'our world' is something outside the divine and comic reality which is in Christ, or that is not already part of the world which is sustained, accepted, and reconciled in Him. It does not mean that one must still begin by applying some kind of 'principle' to our situation and our time. The inquiry is directed rather towards the way in which the reality in Christ, which for a long time already has comprised us and our world within itself, it taking effect as something now present, and towards the way in which life may be conducted in this reality. Its purpose is, therefore, participation in the reality of God and of the world in Jesus Christ today, and this participation must be such that I never experience the reality of God without the reality of the world or the reality of the world without the reality of God." Dietrich Bonhoeffer in *Ethics,* New York and London, 1963, p. 194.

a manner that it will give light to this world and help this changing world to see and to purify its present and emerging values. Moral and dogmatic teaching finally must reach out to man who is still developing, who is a man with social and cosmic dimensions.

We are not imposing here a debatable vision of an indefinite progress in the world. We impose nothing; we only propose an interpretation, a view of faith that relates to the vision of the world which, in fact, men have today.

Men experience the world in a certain way, as a world of unlimited progress, a world which they see as being effectively developed and directed by their own talents and to their own benefit. There is immense research and effort going on which sometimes can confuse our thinking on the other realities, outside the world of "progress." Let the scholars and scientists do their work of scientific examination and statement. Let the theologians make their critical reflections. We, as religious educators, do not, however, necessarily have to take a position on the ultimate meaning of those reflections and statements. What counts for the teachers of the faith is this new way of being in the world, this new sensitivity which is drawing all humanity into the heart of its being. Under the movement of the Spirit, religion teachers find themselves irresistibly drawn not only to the bare statement of the facts, but to the heart of the material, the life of the word they are to give.

We can take here for an example a particularly difficult point: the question of teaching poverty or humility to the adolescent. Young people cannot bear to hear us tell them in the name of Christ, "Be humble," "Be poor," "Renounce yourself," if they identify humility with a lack of prestige and human value, or if they know of no other form of poverty than one which consists in having nothing and living stingily.

When we confront them with these spiritual imperatives, they are all ready to answer that in order to be somebody one needs money, a degree, charm, "pull," a good wardrobe, and so forth. They will tell us that they want to live intensely and that the only way of being recognized and of fulfilling one's desires is to belong to a group, to be able to communicate emotionally with others. They are not necessarily rejecting the evangelical precepts when they say these things; what they are rejecting, however, is the traditional presentation of the precepts that they have been given.

How, then, for example, can poverty be presented? By making the Gospel less forceful? By watering down and softening the words of Christ? No, but by going beyond the words themselves and carefully showing what new ways of expression and realization of these precepts the Spirit is taking today. Evangelical poverty! Must we not today accent that aspect of the teaching in which God is not poor because He owns nothing, but because He gives all? God's poverty is not an absence; God's poverty is not a lack of possessions, for who possesses more than God? But it is an absence of jealousy and egoism and selfishness in possession. The poverty of God! It is to own everything in order to share everything, even his inner life, even His Son Jesus.

The teacher must make young people understand that, while there was a time when frequently poverty was interpreted as an absence of possession, today in a civilization of competition and efficient production we will be poor and detached not by refusing to acquire, but by trying to put our talents in the service of all, and by sharing all in a fraternal fashion.

Adolescents can then be directed—carefully, of course, since it is the task of the Holy Spirit to guide them towards personal concrete ways—towards a poverty which is defined first in terms of sharing, and a sharing in a more and more carefully understood and universal manner.[5]

2. Educating to Christian Fullness

Our second task is concerned more with the method of presenting doctrinal realities to our students. We have called it "educating to Christian fullness" because the emphasis is not on what is divisive in man or extrinsic to him, but rather it is an understanding of, a dialogue with man; it is not concentrating on the evil in man and on his sinfulness, but on his worth.

So the doctrinal message will be presented in an approach that first considers how a particular doctrine is intimately connected with man himself as God made him (the creation aspect), then how that truth transcends and is richer than the individual (the incarnation aspect), and finally how this doctrine is incompatible with or breaks away from or is not part of merely human limitations or weaknesses in human life (the redemption aspect).

Let us take, as a concrete situation, the question of friendship.

5. We are very conscious of not having touched on all the aspects of poverty; however, we only want here to emphasize only one of its aspects as an example of the new direction to be given to its doctrinal presentation.

54

A. FRIENDSHIP IS NATURAL TO MAN AND GOD

We must first make it very clear that God is not against love. The total absorption of an adolescent in friendship is not in itself against Christian life. On the contrary, it is God who puts love in the heart of man; and man, when he loves, should be joyful when God watches him loving. Jesus looks at human friendship with loving eyes and a sympathetic heart. The teacher, like Jesus, must admire his students and must help the students have the proper light on their search for friendship, for love. The teacher must help the adolescents in the questions that arise, the values that must be determined.

B. THE TRANSCENDENCE AND RICHNESS OF MAN'S FRIENDSHIP WITH GOD

To stop at the first level of friendship is totally insufficient for a Christian. We must bring out the radical transcendence, the infinitely more profound dimension that transfigures human friendship when it enters into contact with the Lord of Glory. We are not talking here of breaking away from human friendships; rather, it is a fulfillment of friendship that is a super-elevation, a super-animation. It is a fulfillment that gives a completely unthought-of level and expression of love in friendship. It is the movement from one level of love into a new and infinitely richer one. Love will then find its meaning in relation to the kingdom of God. The experiences of friendship which one has in a personal way will become an entrance and an introduction to the fullness of love which will be realized by the entire community of the risen bodies in Christ.

C. BREAKING AWAY FROM LIMITATIONS AND SIN

The first level, very human, is clear and appealing. The second level, at the age of adolescence, represents the fundamentally positive approach of a dynamic Christian call, and we know that many adolescents are aware of the truth of a full life in the Christian sense.

But we must not forget to stress this third point: Friendship, to be truly Christian and "enter into the glory" must cut itself off from all falseness and all the weakening effects of sin. Hence a clear knowledge of the world of Satan and a real understanding of redemption (which includes suffering and self-giving) must be generously willed by those who want to follow the path of Christ.

What is in man, what is offered to man, and what he must do to best grow in these gifts to him, are the three elements which should be underlying all our teaching. These are three facets of the one approach which should play a vital part in the inner life of our teaching.

1. We begin by speaking of and communicating to the needs and actual life of the adolescent.

2. We then follow by showing, not the evil, but the human insufficiencies of these needs and this life; and we announce, we transmit, we open to them the richness and profound dimensions of the message of good news.

3. Finally, we explain and correct, we guide and help to form.

3. The Place of the Cross in Religious Education

Since we have been following the direction of humanism, who would not wonder about the place of the cross? Are we not running the grave risk that "the cross of Christ be made void" (1 Cor. 1, 17)? Inseparable from the idea of fullness in the redemptive plan, the cross must be clearly central and unifying in our catechetical thinking.

How can we present the cross to young people who are seeking human fullness? We must reflect here on three aspects of the cross and on the manner of giving them in our teaching.

A. THE CROSS AS A LAW OF PROGRESS AND OF BECOMING

It seems very important for us to tell our students that the cross consists above all in an acceptance and acquiescence in ourselves and in the world to the true movement of life. God is directing the world towards fullness, towards abundance, but this necessarily includes suffering, a sign that the world is not yet totally whole and completed. And it is through suffering that God is accomplishing the necessary growth and changes that lead towards fulfillment. Is not death itself the greatest change which leads us to the vision of God? Pain is, in fact, the underlying law of all masterpieces.

On the one hand, we will show that any action, any progress towards a greater and fuller existence must allow for effort and suffering. For example, nothing is more invigorating and yet more troublesome than to follow through to the end of a job, or to be wholly faithful to a friendship, or to a commitment we have made. The more a man submits himself to the law of life and progress, the more he will be provoked, annoyed, exasperated —crucified.

It takes a very profound act of renunciation to submit to the natural laws of growth. One cannot, for example, grow older without having to forego the security that comes from the protective family life, to forego certain forms of friendship, the carefree school life, and so forth, without having to accept the limits and crosses that are part of the more mature life one chooses.

We will tell our students that each time they pass into a new center of existence, a new focal point in life, with the greatest love possible and a true understanding of this new situation, they will receive the grace of being detached from their own fears and false hopes, be rendered more humble and poor (and hence capable of receiving), and be led step by step through unforeseeable paths towards a greater spiritual maturity in this new stage of growth.

On the other hand, we will lead them to foresee, especially if an occasion demands it, that we live in a world grappling with the forces of evil. Going out into the world to live this new life of Christ is not going out into some predisposed, marionetted world. It is impossible to be faithful to life and not to experience a certain number of crucifying failures, compromises, lost opportunities, mediocre successes.

In light of this, we must tell our students that a Christian must then hold with faith to a God who pursues a plan of salvation, of reparation for sin, by ways that are in actuality mysterious to us, sometimes by ways that scandalize us, but which will open up to us a resurrection which is already realized in His Son. In the name of the word of God, we will announce the paradoxical, contradictory certitudes of the Beatitudes.

Concretely we will try to make ours, to the greatest extent possible at any one time in our lives, this cross which falls on us; and we will say that, if we have to carry it, it is in order that great joy and abundance of life may come, "For I reckon the sufferings of the present time are not worthy to be compared with the glory to come that will be revealed in us."

This submission to reality, even when it baffles us, is very important, for it will lead us to an abundance of life. We will have to accept death in the name of life. By our (paradoxical) life-giving acceptance, we are allowing the hand of God to form us even to eternity. By it we are entering with Christ the Redeemer into God's plan in history, and we permit the Spirit to come a little more into this world until the final transformation comes.

While we accept, in this imperfect world and imperfect human nature, the presence and necessity of suffering, we will try, however, to make our students understand with all our power and determination that we ourselves are engaged in the struggle to suppress evil or, as the case may be, to help those who suffer to overcome with Christ their hardships and emerge victorious. We will challenge our students to a new way of life which brings them away from any empty and easy way of avoiding suffering in themselves and others. They must discover that the only authentic barrier to evil is a courageous stand with those who, with Christ, have decided to multiply love and progress in the world, even at the cost of suffering.

B. THE CROSS AS A LAW OF OPENING TO THE GOSPEL AND TO OTHERS

The world today, as we have said, is totally centered on its full development. In such a context, should not the cross be placed in the center of this dimension? The cross should consist less in the flight from the world than in the quality of a life within this world.

The cross, law of opening to the Gospel:

Formerly, we thought that the adolescent could best develop his personality by imitating leaders and by following the success stories given by our society. We asked him to become someone. We would tell him: Be successful!

In this view, discipline, self-control, study all types of natural asceticism, were considered means, sometimes demanding, for acquiring the ideal personality; they included mortification and penance (of a type) which were seen as the means of constructing and developing one's self and also forming his will.

In a world less marked by the necessity of reproducing and imitating behavior patterns of another generation than by a need of increasing and adapting oneself in new fashion, the problem of the cross and of ascetics poses completely different problems. In past times, the Christian could sometimes borrow patterns of growth from the culture in which he lived, whose emphasis was on tradition, imitation, established values. Now the Christian, raised in a new world, must see the cross and asceticism in a new way. It is important here that we learn to accept a cross which makes us always open and adaptable to a world which is in continuous change. The question is: How?

It can be done, first of all, by being willing at all times to face up to our own lives and to the work we do, and to see it all in terms of the word of God. This seems to be our key to the problem. To accept the cross is to will the constant modification of ourselves and, if necessary, an upheaval of the values in the world around us, by allowing the clear light of the word of God to affect us.

Let us take an example. At a meeting, the members of a group try to work out the program for the year. Most everyone wants to draw back when they think of the work involved in order for the planned program to be implemented. What is necessary in this case is the willingness of the individual to accept the discipline needed in terms of his time and talent. He will have to learn to organize his time methodically, to give of himself in the completion of the work. Yet he must also learn to be open to changes that may arise, and to be prepared to follow into new areas in which God may call him. His cross is to be ready to place himself at the disposal of others, even at a cost to himself.

So our life will be doubly confronted by the word of God: we are not only called by the word, but we must be prepared to organize and discipline ourselves according to what the word demands of us. To accept the cross is to be open to what the Gospel asks of us.

Is this not, then, an approach to the discovery of the real sense of Christian asceticism?

If, for example, a man does not smoke because it is harmful to his health, that is a case of purely natural asceticism. However, Christian asceticism is not shown by actions that a man decides on his own to do in order to improve, develop, or correct something in himself; rather, it is a *passion* in the sense of an act by which one passes into God, allows oneself to be remade by him, to be mortified by His infinite generosity. (The idea is that a passion is something we go through, something which displaces us. We have here the idea of the passover, which implies a passing

61

through, a break, a displacement, a movement on the way to some place.)

Christian asceticism, then, is the act of exposing oneself to the fire and light of God, an act by which we become caught up into His infinite life which opens to us perspectives we could not dream of. Though in allowing ourselves to be remade by God, we die to certain seemingly precious parts of ourselves because of a fullness of life which is greater and richer than our own: the pouring forth of the paschal richness of the Gospel.

We will have to find ways of renunciation for our students, ways of sacrifice that will make them open to the word of God, and help them to hear and appreciate one another. We will bring them, perhaps, to plan for periods of intense spiritual life at certain times when they can experience true fasting, in the literal sense or in the wider sense of some type of restraint, in order that they can come to know that it is God above all who makes them live and that it is from Him alone that we look for our daily bread, which is to do His will. It will be in setting some special time to search the Scriptures, to hear them, that the students may be able to find that, in giving of their time, they have found that the living God is the bread of life, a source of life above and beyond all human joys.

The cross, the law of opening to others:

Along with the cross of truly accepting the Gospel message, the greatest cross that is offered us is that of meeting our fellow men. We live in a world where human relations are more and more numerous, varied, heterogeneous. We should accept these encounters with our brothers; and the openness it requires of us (as a providential cross given to us so often) is our best chance to discover the real face of God: ". . . as you did it to one of the least of these my brethren, you did it to me" (Mt. 25, 40).

As a result, we must educate our students to that great source of asceticism of our day which is group living, group discussion, and action in community or team work.

C. THE CROSS AS A SCANDAL AND A MYSTERY

Finally, we come to that aspect of the cross which touches the deep, profound mystery of redemption. The cross can present itself in a form that represents or causes moral destruction in some persons, even spiritual decay that is so great that it will seem radically to diminish a person and have him rejected as contemptible by society, brutally destroying all that constituted the quality of his life or even his reason for living. These are the scandals of all times, and scandals felt more deeply today in a world exclusively centered on earthly success.

The Gospel shows us in Jesus Christ how God can drive a man as far as that in order to make reparation through Him for the boundless evils of the world and for the arrogant pretensions of man wanting to master his own destiny and assume responsibility for his salvation.

With adolescents, however, we should be very careful and merciful as we initiate them to the profound and disconcerting mystery of the cross. Jesus did not inconsiderately announce Gethsemane to His disciples. Like the disciples, young people are still in that situation where Gethesemane is too much to bear; they are still on the threshold of full growth in the Spirit. This is not to say, of course, that there are not some adolescents who have had a very intense experience of the cross. Some of them are born and raised in an environment or family dominated by suffering. These are students who have been specially blessed by God, who are specially in the care of the Spirit; and it is our task to direct this fecund experience of theirs in such a way that they will know it is a gift of God, a special invitation to His kingdom.

The *kairos* of each student will some day come. It will come in the form of a cross, as a mystery, something demanding great courage and love of God. Let us, therefore, never suggest that the cross of Jesus Christ was some far-off event that happened in history; rather, we must teach them that it is something which may come tomorrow, —indeed, something which may already be happening. The cross is not something to look back at, but to await.

A religious-education program, therefore, which is directed towards human fullness is not an easy approach. For it may very well be that it is necessary to suffer greatly in order truly to love the world with peace of soul and simplicity of heart. Perhaps it is necessary to go through much anguish and difficulty in order to be definitely optimistic about the ultimate worth of human fullness. The teacher who does not live the realities of the world in Jesus Christ—in other words, sharing His cross—will never fully love the world.

And do we dare to deny that adolescents today are awaiting such a teacher?

4. REFLECTIONS

1. What is the style of life in the adult Christian community (the teachers, parents, the environment, the clergy)?

a. Is it a youth approach, one that believes in life, loves the world, that moves forth with life?

b. Is this approach, this style of Christian life, using all the techniques necessary for our age; that is, does it put to use the best among contemporary values and insights? Is it optimistic about man and the world, certain that answers to their problems can be found?

2. Is it evident that our catechetical method witnesses to God's respect, esteem, and admiration for man?

a. Is it a method which begins by dialoguing with all human values before it proposes the message of divine life and redemption?

b. Does it search for new styles and new forms of human life in order to *reveal* them, that is, to uncover their positive aspects, to deepen and enlighten them by relevation, and to purify them?

III.

THE MEANING
OF LIFE TODAY

In order that the message be seen as good news, it will have to be presented to the students as something which gives light to their own experiences and which helps them discover the meaning of life.

The catechetical formation of our students will give meaning to their lives only insofar as the doctrinal presentation and the language used are renewed and rethought according to the thought patterns of the students and their own vision of the world. To this end, catechesis will make use of modern anthropology and the privileged situations of today's youth.[1]

1. THE PROBLEM

Why do our students have so much difficulty in seeing the message of Christ as good news?

1. By "privileged situations" we mean those situations which make a person sensitive and open to a particular subject, a particular point of view, or a particular expression of language. It can be a situation which is an occasion for reflection, which can lead a person to think, which can be revealing of truth.

Everyone agrees that revelation should and can be an experience of happiness and joy, of a full rich life with God, and all agree that revelation should be given as good news. But how to achieve these goals is the critical question. What should we stress, what words are we to use if our catechetical programs are to be the source of good news? This third chapter will try to point out some of the principal areas in the problem of the transmission of the word.

Which one of us hasn't suffered pangs of conscience when we have realized that the realities concerning the God of Jesus Christ lead only to boredom and indifference on the part of a great many adolescents. Who has not been told by some student, "You're not telling us anything that makes sense," or, "It's a lot of words. That's not for real," or, "Religious instruction is a waste of time."

Some student has put it this way: "When you talk of how the world looks at the Church, how it judges it, then you are asking real questions. Everybody listens. But all of a sudden, you start giving a spiel on the 'nature of the Church.' What difference does that make? It's hard to listen for more than five minutes."

Our presentation of the word of Christ does not interest adolescents. It has become a timeless *in se* which reveals nothing to them. It is eternal truth which stands outside of their lives, and is of no real concern in their lives. "What does it do for me when you tell me there are two natures in Jesus Christ?" And yet we know that many of these young people have an authentic faith, a truly good will. Then what is happening?

Essentially this: We are revealing nothing to them because the truth we claim to announce to them is not made part of them; it remains outside of them. When we tell them that God is incarnate and saves, it doesn't have anything to do with their lives. The revelation opens nothing for them. There is no revelation here for the good reason that we do not reveal to them that they exist in Christ. We speak to them of other things, but we do not give them the insights they need.

To reveal to the adolescent, to open up truth for him and to open him to the truth, the catechesis must be expressive of the whole man as he is today.

For our religious education to be truly revealing, it is necessary that it show Christ as the revelation of the Father and Christ as a light for man and within man. Our catechesis should help the student to discover himself while at the same time showing Christ in him.[2] Karl Rahner has defined this affirmation in theological terms:

Our preaching is not really an indoctrination with something alien from outside but the awakening of something within, as yet not understood but nevertheless really present; . . . any communication of Christianity is always a communication of what is already there, alive, within a man. And if it often seems to be otherwise: if people get the impression that we are preaching a very extraordinary, remote doctrine, intelligible only to experts, which no normal man could find interesting unless he stopped being an ordinary man, it is not because Christianity is really like this but because we have not rightly understood it. We have only half grasped it, and instead of the other, equally necessary, half we fall back on the power of tradition, which still, perhaps, works effectively for us, so that we think it is bound to be just as convincing for everybody else and are highly astonished when this is not so.[3]

2. Yves Congar writes: "The Bible is not a theology for man, it is an anthropology for God."
3. *The Christian Commitment,* New York, 1963, p. 103.

This is a major text for catechetics. There can be no revelation of God if man is not also revealed to himself.

Now this supposes that the language and the doctrinal points of view are those of man today.

In order for religious education to reveal to students today the richness of the message of Christ, it must first and by definition be expressive of and organized about what exists in man, what is lived and felt by him today. For the message can be revelation only if, in these times, we renew the doctrinal presentation in terms of the people we are talking to.

Today to speak of death to a 15-year-old boy as the separation of the body from the soul, or to talk of the nature and consubstantiality of the divine persons in the Trinity is to condemn one's own efforts, at least at the beginning of the contact. It is to reveal nothing at all. Adolescents today do not feel or do not express their experience or death or of revelation in such terms.[4] The presentation of content may be materially exact, but it is, in its form, unfaithful to catechetics considered in its connection with revelation. To lift a veil off "nothing" that is meaningful to the student is to unveil or reveal "nothing" to him.

On the contrary, if we begin by the experience that an adolescent has had of death, if we talk of the Christian sense of death, if we define Christian death from what he has lived, then we have a chance of revealing to him. This youth has heard songs about separation. He knows what it means to lose a friend, to fail in something, to be sick, to miss an exam; he has learned that going away on a trip where he will be far from familiar surroundings,

4. We want to insist on the fact that we must not condemn such terms, such presentations. We only want to reserve them to theology or to a later stage of doctrinal presentation.

moving from city to city, leaving friends, can be dying a little. This is in his life, his language. He does not think of death in terms of a separation of body and soul.

It is the student's language and life, in other words, that must be unveiled so that the truths implicitly contained in his life and language may be shown to him. It is his experience of death that must be revealed to him, summoned forward in the name of God. Maybe then will we define the Christian sense of death, but in a manner different from that of the preceding century. For example, death can be understood as the ultimate act by which man abandons his earthly forms of action and presence to the world to the power of the Spirit of God, in order to acquire in the Risen Christ a new and more dynamic source of action and communion.

Can it be said that the doctrine has changed? Certainly not! But what has changed is the older method of presenting death. We have departed in some ways from the traditional approach, but we have also taken some older elements from the teaching of the Church—for example, the ideas contained in the preface of the Mass of the dead.

It is not, then, a question of "adjusting" doctrine, any more than it is a question of criticizing earlier forms of doctrine—they revealed to men in their own times. It is not a question of letting the treasure of earlier formulas and doctrinal and moral presentations fall away; they will always be necessary, in any good catechesis, to give the proper nuances to difficult points or to give a theological formulation of a mystery. Who will pretend to reach or to transmit the spirit without the letter? The first point of catechesis, however, is not to repeat the forms and the words used for another generation, but it is to reveal Christ today.

Religious education does not reveal today, for it has slowly evolved towards indoctrinating rather than vivifying.

Through carelessness, through a need for security in terms of set formulas and rites, through laziness perhaps, we have slowly lost the very sense of religious education. We have taken the old words, the teaching structures, the forms of transmission of the Middle Ages, and we have presented them to the men of our time. It is the same in the case of the vocabulary of the Gospel and that of the whole Bible. To be able to resort to the words of the Gospel in an effective way we must uncover their revealed content and translate it into the language of today, —for example, the terms "justice" and "peace." We have gone, without being aware of it, from an authentic catechesis that was an historical continuation of the revelation brought about by and in Jesus Christ to a religious instruction that is an accumulation of words having no antecedent in life.

2. THE ELEMENTS OF THIS APPROACH

We will try to be more precise in what we mean when we say that there must be a renewal in doctrinal presentation and language. It is extremely important, especially in view of the work that is at stake and in view of the risks that must be taken on this difficult path.

1. Doctrinal Renewal

By renewal of the doctrinal presentation we understand two main points:

A. A RENEWAL OF THE APPROACH OF SYNTHESIS

In suggesting the use of synthesis, we mean by that to bring together certain aspects or points of the faith into clearer relationships. Thus we will organize the different parts of the doctrine we want to teach around a theme or a particular point of view that will throw more light on certain sections and less on others.

For example, here are two possible programs on the Church.

The first outline is taken from a standard book on Catholic doctrine published in the second decade of this century:

1. The Catholic Church:

—its institution,

—its distinctive marks,

—absence of these marks in the Protestant and Greek churches,

—necessity of belonging to the Church,

—meaning of the expression "Outside the Church there is no salvation."

2. Constitution of the Church:

—its hierarchy,

—its powers,

—the pope,

—the pope's primacy, his infallibility,

—the bishops,

—the rights of the Church,

—the relation of Church and state.

The second outline is directly inspired by the conciliar draft of Vatican II on the Church:

1. The Church, mystery and sacrament visibly and efficiently revealing, although in veiled form, the plan of God to save all men.

2. The people of God on the march, a people that comprises all those—clergy and laity—who are incorporated by their baptism in Christ.

3. Hierarchy, a service of the people of God, with responsibilities and powers corresponding to their burden to nourish, to organize, and to lead the Christian people.

4. The laity, and their participation in the life of the Church by being involved in the life of the world; co-participating in the sacerdotal, prophetic, and royal missions of Jesus Christ.

5. Holiness: God Himself communicates His holiness and calls all men to holiness—bishops, priests, faithful—because He loves them. Bishops, priests, and faithful are united by love.

6. Religious: a particular gift to the life of the Church, devoted to the welfare of the whole Church.

7. The pilgrim Church—the accomplishment of the work of Christ will take place "when all will be consummated" and all the saints will be the glory of God in Christ.

8. The Virgin Mary, mother of the Son of God made man, and associated with His work by her free consent in faith and charity.

The second example shows us how the idea of synthesis can make doctrinal presentation more meaningful for and relevant to contemporary man. In catechetics the task today will be to make our presentations based on a synthesis of the faith (an approach made possible by the Council), and to make them consonant with the synthetical perception of the world that men of today have.

It is such a renewal of the idea of synthesis that Gabriel Moran proposes in his book *Catechesis of Revelation*. "The whole of man's world is expressive of God's revelation in Christ," Brother Moran writes. "Nothing of itself is guaranteed to be a revelatory instrument, but everything by the grace of God has become capable of being revelatory of the Christian God. This fact opens unlimited possibilities for the teaching of Christian revelation. When it is proposed that the grace of Christ is awakened by the catechist's words, this does not mean that it is only 'religious' concepts and words which are in question. Any words, ideas, pictures, or experiences which create the possibility of deep personal reflection can have a place in catechetical instruction. Words and activities with no apparent religious orientation may be all the more powerful by reason of the indirectness of the appeal."[5]

B. A DISCOVERY OF THE AREAS COMMON TO REVELATION AND CONTEMPORARY MAN

In all areas of religious education it is important that the teacher be aware of the present scene and understand how much of what the student is living or experiencing is part of God's revelation about man. He must see that the student is involved, even if unknowingly, in the realities of the faith we are talking about— the Exodus, sacrifice, new life. It is a very necessary condition, as we have said, for revealing to them the reality of the message. It is the opening through which God comes to them.

The educator must fill his catechetical approach with the forms of the Christian life that the student consciously or unconsciously lives already. He must address himself to the very things in life that the student is reacting to and those areas that the adolescent is sensitive to. Such must be our own research. An analysis of the student's mentality can help. This, however, must never be

5. In *Catechesis of Revelation*, New York and London, 1966, p. 135.

considered as a technique to interest the audience who want to talk about themselves, but it must be an encounter with different forms of life and a discovery for the catechist of the spontaneous reactions of students through which he can then speak.

Examples:

—How does today's society live the mystery of the Exodus? In the frequent moving from area to area, in the problem of urban renewal, in the insecurity of a sickness, in the misery of slums. That is, the Exodus today in concrete realities—people forced to leave, to go beyond themselves, to abandon themselves to someone greater who will save them "with hands and arms outstretched."

—How does the unbeliever live the sacrifice and death that Christ Himself went through? In the accepted experience of a departure, or a death, or oppressive working conditions.

—How does such a group as the one I have in my class live today the eternity of heaven? In an experience of love that shortens time and gives the impression that hours are but seconds, in the experience of a certain human fullness.

2. The Renewal of Language

Doctrinal presentation and language are inseparable. The language is the man. Those who give tests are well aware of this fact. A renewed doctrinal presentation cannot exist without a new language, just as there can be no soul without a body.

By renewal of language, we must understand the *aggiornamento* of our system of verbal expression in religious education. The verbal expression of our catechetical approach must catch up to the authentic verbal expression of young people today. The vocabulary of religion class must express the reality of the student's life and experiences.

A. THE IMPORTANCE OF LANGUAGE IN RELIGIOUS EDUCATION

Language, in fact, is very different from a series of words. Nothing is more impersonal, more neutral, than mere words. Like music, language is essentially rhythm, movement, a matter of accent and emphasis and shading, associations, groupings of certain words and phrases, new insights from new sensitivities and personal growth. Language is as rich, as varied, as complex as life itself, of which it is the expression.

Also, if we consider language as "the best tool to understand the world and to dominate it," we will understand how each person, each generation of men, is forced to make the traditional heritage of language more precise, even to inventing new modes of expression in proportion to a new comprehension of the world. Language is the bearer of all the dimensions of man, his ambitions, his discoveries, and his conquests. Thus we can perceive what an error we would commit in reducing to the aridity of a list of mere words and expressions the overflowing abundance of language.

But a student may have this to say of his teacher: "He's talking our language, but it's not us." Language is much more than sound. It has to become familiar, off-hand, a part of one's daily routine, expressive of one's way of doing things and looking at life. It is a world of nuance, reflection, unpremeditated response. It is evolutionary, capable of growing, and itself an important factor in the development of one's personality. It is a way of apprehending reality and possessing the world. Above all else, therefore, it must be natural; affected language will be immediately condemned for what it is: unreal.

Can we talk to our students, therefore, of the body which will be glorified in the New Jerusalem in such terms as "impassibility" or "subtility"? In view of their own experiences, what can such language mean?

Finding a new language for them will require that we uncover the experiences, the mental concepts, the images by which they have some notion of a "spiritual body." A rich human experience, a time of complete exhilaration, of domination over physical obstacles such as is felt in diving or running or after climbing a mountain or playing a basketball game, perhaps one of these will help the student understand. For another, it might be the experience of perfect physical coördination and control of the body in dance. To a third it might be an experience in which the body almost impossibly overcomes natural laws, as in the high jump.

A friend of ours once remarked, "One day I was watching a young boy who was learning to play the trumpet. After a half hour of practicing he stopped and said, 'How exasperating it is to have an instrument and not be able to put into it all that you feel. I would like to be like the musician I saw last night on TV. He made himself one with his trumpet. He had something to say in his heart, and it came out of his horn. He could say anything he wanted with it.'" Well, the resurrected body will be like that well-played horn, a body perfectly docile to all our loving intentions, a body made for total communion.

We are not advocating here a radical suppression of all traditional language, but we will place them at the end of our teaching preferably, after the "revelation" as a point of reference, as a precise statement, sometimes as an easily remembered formula. In speaking to our students, we will begin by a language that reveals, that opens, a language that expresses for them the themes of revelation that are a part of them, and that we must draw out through the communication of language.

3. SOME NECESSARY CONSIDERATIONS

Two elements control the renewal of doctrinal presentations and language: the understanding and use of anthropology, and the privileged situations of young people, that is, those experiences which make our students open to a particular subject, point of view, or language.

A renewal of the doctrinal presentation and of theological language cannot be done through anything but man, and man in his actual existence. And it seems to us that it is by reference to anthropology and the privileged situations of the lives of young people that the renewal can best be helped because it is in these areas that we best find the living man. Anthropology will give us the sense and the permanent dimensions of man; the privileged situations of the lives of young people, especially our own students, will give us the actual and current burning issues, the live thinking on sensitive areas of their world.

But these terms, no doubt, lack precision. They are more or less new terms, more or less in the current thinking, yet terms indicating rather fundamental methods and ways of seeing.

1. Anthropology

Today anthropology is a science which tends to include all the sciences of man.[6] As it relates to religious education, we conceive of it along the lines of a science which instructs us on the fundamental dimensions of man, on the categories by which he discovers himself and expresses himself historically. Well understood, and with more development in the field, anthropology should furnish us with the general manner of speaking humanly of divine "things" and divinely of human "things."

Thus modern anthropology spontaneously gives us a definition of man different from that of the Middle Ages, namely, that "man is a reasonable being, composed of body and soul," a definition which brought together the categories which man at that time used in his discovery of himself.

Marcel van Caster, on the contrary, proposes the following definition of man-in-situation, according to contemporary philosophical anthropology: "A free being who develops in the world for the sake of the communion of persons: called to live in union with God: moving towards a positive surpassing of temporal existence." And he adds, "Catechesis must certainly hand on as unchangeable what, in fact, belongs to revealed truth, but if it is to be faithful to divine revelation, constantly calling man to what surpasses him, it will take care that its approach and expressions do not 'reduce' truth to what a single point of view, and expressions as limited as that point of view, discover in revelation."[7]

6. See Karl Rahner's definition of "Anthropology" in his *Theological Dictionary,* New York and London, 1965.

7. *The Structure of Catechetics,* New York and London, 1965, pp. 142, 132.

2. Privileged Situations

In referring constantly to the "privileged situations" in the lives of adolescents, we can make the doctrinal presentation and the language more concrete and effective. We call "privileged situations" those situations which render one sensitive to a particular subject, a particular point of view, a particular language.

We can take an example that sets off the value and role of anthropology and privileged situations. The death of President John F. Kennedy became in many adolescents a privileged situation, in the sense that this sudden and catastrophic death made them very sensitive to the subject of death, and death conceived as a personal phenomenon. How many teachers used this opportunity to study the subject of death and to present it in light of the problems faced by the students on the question of Kennedy's death, which was seen not as a transformation but as a limitation and a scandal?

In this case, the privileged situation would have furnished the subject, the point of view, the form of expression, the images, the emotional content which could prepare and help the students grasp the revelation contained in it. We must stress the importance of these privileged situations for the religious education of the adolescent. Whether they are caused by environment, a special event, or a psychological development as can result from a critical juvenile friendship, these privileged situations contain a kind of calling of God to revelation. To pass them over is to refuse to tell the good news to the poor; to answer these situations is to reveal, and this revelation is the supreme opening of the Gospel, of the good news, of the kingdom.

These privileged situations which show contemporary sensitivity to a particular area of concern are not only lived but are also spoken about, expressed. When they are expressed, it is in a language that reveals a certain concept of man, his historical situation, his social relations. There is a meeting place, a joining between anthropology as a science of man expressing himself socially and historically, and the privileged situations in which he discovers and expresses himself.

Let us take another possible example. In the past few years there have been several violent, emotionally laden incidents in the civil-rights movement, for example the Watts riot, the shooting of James Meredith in his march through Mississippi, the earlier violence in Birmingham when teenagers were pushed back by fire hoses, and the riots in the summer of 1966 in Chicago, Cleveland, Dayton, and other urban centers. These events, especially Watts, Birmingham, and Chicago, in which adolescents were involved in the actions themselves, were openings for the students to reveal their own ideas on man, human fullness, justice, love. From these the teacher could reveal the good news in terms closely related to the coming of the kingdom. A difficult task? Yes! But a necessary one, especially if we want our students to discover the good news in the world they live in, and how the good news is meant to be lived.

4. THE NECESSITY OF RENEWAL IN PRESENTATION AND LANGUAGE

Why is such a renewal of doctrinal presentation and language so urgently required?

1. The General Theme: Our Message Must Be Good News for Today

Why this *aggiornamento*? Why an *aggiornamento* which should be permanent in the Church? We have already said why: because there is no good news if man is not concerned, if it does not reveal man, open man to himself and to God. There is no good news if man is not revealed, that is to say, if his needs are not satisfied, if he himself is not restored with infinite life, if he is not corrected, guided, saved. But he will not have a true communion with revelation if the doctrinal presentation we make does not come to grips with the concrete human reality, if it does not express human reality, if it speaks a language other than that of today's man. We have nothing against the language of the Middle Ages. In fact, we admire it greatly, for it represents an extraordinary effort. But it expressed and revealed the Middle Ages. Each period must have its own language; otherwise man will be betrayed and revelation will be impossible.

To the question why such a renewal is so urgently required we answer:

—by reason of today's youth;

—by reason of the requirements of the world in which they live now and will live in the future.

2. The Problem: Crisis of Faith

Young people today are threatened by a crisis of faith. The world and man's vision of the world are going through extraordinary and very rapid changes. If we still maintain the doctrinal presentation and catechetical language of centuries gone by, or in some cases of several previous generations, we should not be astonished to witness a massive exodus from the Church. The Gospel for the twentieth century cannot be placed in old containers from the sixteenth century. Youth will be incapable of either understanding or living the message of Christ with our old doctrinal presentation.

Faith is, as we have said, adherence to Christ, participation in His insights and thought; but His light to men is in time. It touches man only in the extension of the incarnation of the word of God in time. It can express itself only in the signs, images, and mental structures of an age whose values and points of view it adapts and uses.

We would be risking an unbearable breaking away and crisis of faith if men today could think about their beliefs and express them and account for them only in concepts and forms of a previous age. We would also run the risk of not catechizing at all, because we would not be opening them to truth, not revealing truth because we would not be revealing anything. It would be the same as giving a remarkable speech in Greek to people who understand only English. As perfect as the speech might be, it would say nothing.

Is this not what is happening today? When young people talk of their difficulty in believing in heaven or hell, are they really rebelling against the reality of heaven or hell? Or, on the contrary, are they rebelling against the way we have expressed these revelations, which have become meaningless to them because of our language?

When students express their difficulties in living as Christians, their problems of thinking about the world and the flow of life stated in some of their religion books, can we accuse them of bad faith or ill will? Are they opposing the message of Christ or simply a certain interpretation of His message which was elaborated at a given period to solve the problem of individual salvation and perfection for that day?

The words of John XXIII show us the direction we must take: "The Christian, Catholic, and apostolic spirit of the whole world expects a step forward towards a doctrinal penetration and a formation of consciousness in faithful and perfect conformity to the authentic doctrine, which, however, should be studied and expounded through the methods of research and through the literary forms of modern thought. The substance of the ancient doctrine of the deposit of faith is one thing, and the way in which it is presented is another. And it is the latter that must be taken into great consideration, with patience if necessary, everything being measured in the forms and proportion of a magisterium which is predominantly pastoral in character."[8]

5. CONCLUSION

This is an immense and daring job, for our time is rich with new acquisitions and filled with social and human upheaval. Who will dare to declare himself the one to transmit the faith, to make it part of the thinking and sensitivity of our age? Who today can pretend to penetrate with Christ's eternal way of seeing all the actual richness of the personalist, existentialist, scientific, and technical mind of today? It is not an easy task, and no one man

8. From his address given at the opening of the Council; see *The Documents of Vatican II*, New York, 1966, p. 715.

can do it. In many countries courageous theologians are working at it; their researches, which have given new breathing power to Christian thought, will be called on to give life to religious education also. And Vatican II has, in a decisive manner, pointed out to us the will and the ways of the Spirit for our time.

Who would not acknowledge this? In these times we cannot leave our students alone to build by themselves their own synthesis of faith according to forms and formulas too remote for their mentality. It is important, therefore, that teachers help the students to purify the images and signs which bring the message to young people, to formulate anew their faith, and to engage them in a Christian view of God's plan and of the realities of the world, all this according to the genius of their age. In a word, we cannot afford to fake our way through a religion course, handily peppering an old, borrowed language with the latest jargon. There can be no virtuoso catechizing. For Jesus has confided to us the work of giving the good news to our students.

6. REFLECTIONS

To prepare for meetings or sessions with our students, we must begin by discovering the thinking, the sensitive areas, the privileged situations and language which are part of the adolescent's world and which underlie the particular doctrine we are going to talk about.

We will try to discover how the individual youth, the group, gang, clique, class, even ourselves as teachers, best live such a doctrinal message. How do we understand it, feel it, spontaneously express it implicitly or explicitly?

1. Have the students do a research paper on how popular

speech, modern philosophies, the film arts express contemporary thinking on a particular subject; for example, regularly read *Time, Life, Seventeen, Sports Illustrated,* student magazines on the high-school and college levels, for comments on death, friendship, morality, community. How well do current songs, bestsellers, the Sunday magazine sections express the students' feelings about life? Perhaps the students could conduct a "symposium" on contemporary thought, with one student giving a paper on the film, another on magazines, and so forth; with a general discussion following.

2. Have the students read selected passages in the Bible, rich in their own anthropology. What specific insight was given the Jews on man by revelation? Such a study would be richer for a catechetical approach than a study of classical theology, for the Bible has existential categories consonant with the modern world, whereas Scholastic theology has essentialist categories too remote from actual day-to-day thought.

PART TWO

RELIGIOUS EDUCATION

Preparation for Today's World

IV.

FREEDOM IN FAITH

The aim of the teacher will be to lead the adolescents to re-create, to invent[1] their own vision of faith, and to deepen it so that they can truly meet the new and challenging situations in a world more and more in change.

To this purpose the teacher will have to help his students acquire a personal principle of doctrine, dogma rooted in their very lives, rather than dogmatic formulas. He will help his students have basic principles and insights that the students themselves can use to perceive and evaluate the situations they are in. He will thus have to adopt a pedagogy of invention (a teaching which opens the student to search for meaning) rather than one of teacher transmission (one in which the teacher hands down a collection of truth formulated and defined). Finally, he will have to train his students to approach this world in terms of its ultimate meaning, and not to stop at the organizational or functional level of life.

1. Of course, it is not a question here of saying that our students "invent" their faith since we understand it is a gift of God. Faith is not an invention, a finding, of man. But we mean that the same gift of their faith should push the adolescents to a deeper understanding of the content, the practical applications, the forms and expression in their meetings with the world. Youth doesn't invent faith, but it should be "inventive" in its faith, creators of the ways of making it more personal, relevant, and interior. To this idea of "invention" the teacher of religion must lead them.

1. THE MEANING AND NECESSITY OF THIS APPROACH

Why this new understanding of religious teaching? Why aim (in our catechetical approach) at giving adolescents elements that will make them capable, at their level of faith, of inventing and thinking rather than just reproducing the ideas of their teachers? Two factors motivate such an approach and make it urgent:

The increasing change and tempo of the world demand a creative faith, a faith capable of adapting itself and not only of meeting the world with preconceived attitudes and answers; we need a faith capable of growing with change and not only of referring all questions to the letter of the law.

A highly developed level of conscience and freedom demands that men today live their faith not in terms of the existence of God and the traditional Christian values of a particular society, but in a more and more active, demanding, and profound meeting with the universe and modern man as he is found everywhere.

The change in the world, the new freedom, —these are the two factors whose implications and consequences we must consider in the plan of faith.

1. Life of Faith and Change in the Modern World

Let us take an example from the difficulties of an adult Christian active in a parish organization. He talks in the following vein: "For the last few years, I have been completely bewildered. I have been active in the Holy Name Society. The hierarchy gives me the impression of completely disregarding that organization. I do some other work in the Confraternity of Christian Doctrine, but I have the impression we are not making any progress. I've had enough of ready-made slogans like 'you must take an active part in parish work,' etc. Moreover, the priests don't agree among themselves. Some are for the new, some for the old; some for lay participation in all things, others for none. Let them get together first. Then they can tell us what we have to do."

What do such comments reveal? Essentially two things:

1. *The inability of a man to face a situation by himself,* to draw back for a better look, and to decide by himself the best approach. Such is the case of men who in their professional lives never cease to adapt themselves, to make decisions, to face the future; but in their specific life of faith they are at a loss, they are disconcerted, incapable of autonomous decision and creativity.

2. *A constant need to refer oneself to authority.* This indicates that some Christians use authority not only to gain the elements of judgment and the assistance of orthodox thinking on their conduct—which would be an indication of mature thinking— but even more, put themselves in a dependency relation on authority, which then becomes, in fact, the creative source of their action. This is a paradoxical situation, of course, since in their professional lives these men will use their intelligence to find solutions to their day-to-day problems; on the other hand, in their life of faith, they act as though there were no Holy Spirit to help them create, invent their own vision of faith and to discover their own forms of Christian living.[2]

2. And so these men reflect in their actions attitudes which are often adolescent. On the one hand, they have had enough of action under the direction of an authority which they depended upon. On the other hand, although they want freedom, they do not engage in a planned Christian

91

Of course, such a relationship to authority is perhaps not very common. But is there not a relation, a direct connection, between this kind of relationship and the one lived by the majority of adolescents after they have completed their formal religious training? Their life of faith is not adjusted to their daily life; they are for one reason or another unable to adapt themselves and to create their own life of faith and action away from the leader. There is also their almost instinctive reaction against authority joined to a strange dependence on that same authority. What happens when a teenager tries to adjust his life of faith to the world he finds around him and awaiting him?

Youth enters the world with the principles we have taught them and a good knowledge of Christian dogmas, but they are unable to reconcile these principles and ideas to the situations they find themselves in. On the one hand, there are principles, learnedness; and, on the other hand, there is life, reality. Will we argue that youth do not know their religion, that they have some evil propensity to sin? That would be too simple. In fact, generally they are individuals of good will, having acquired a real religious formation and culture; but this formation does not give them a grasp of reality, a hold on the world; it does not render them capable of adjusting their life of faith to a new situation.

The reason is that a student's life of faith cannot grow in a world of change and everyday crises when he has been given for the development of his faith a collection of pre-fabricated solutions, rules-of-thumb which are to apply to each and every situation of his life. Such a ready-made program, no longer a viable one for the student's life of faith, will sooner or later fail

---

action unless an authority decides for them the form and manner suitable for the needed action.

the student, go bankrupt because that is what it is: empty. The Christian student will go into the world like an athlete trained for baseball going into a football game. Not only the rules, but the games themselves are different. In this case, the athlete may "invent" a performance, but not for very long. True invention and initiative require first of all solid preparation and training.

2. Life of Faith and Maturity in Freedom

Another factor forces us to invent, to create our life of faith. It is that modern man and society enjoy a more mobile and autonomous state of freedom.

Man has a new relation to society and nature, and his notion of freedom has therefore changed. Human freedom today depends less on nature and the traditions of a particular society, and is now more concerned with our personal reactions to nature and society. We are no longer formed so much by traditional forms; now we make our own personal reactions to them. We are passing, so to speak, from the freedom of children and adolescents to the freedom of young adults, to a freedom of men who feel themselves responsible.

That is why, leaving our traditional concepts of freedom and control imposed by nature and society, our new sense of freedom suddenly calls us to superimpose our own image on nature, to bring nature to serve our needs instead of adjusting ourselves to nature. And it is henceforth in this approach to nature that we will find our freedom. At the sociological level it is the same; we are not free just because we assume on a world-wide level the traditions and attitudes imposed by a particular culture or civilization. Man is now called to make a clear choice in the confusion of many traditions and opinions in a pluralistic society.

Now in this view of man's state, what will become of the faith? In earlier times, man nourished his faith in the contemplation of nature and in accord with the rhythm of the way of life that surrounded him and supported him. But recently, becoming independent of the natural life about him, and at times in conflict with the idea of nature's control, man must now develop his faith within the framework of his newly acquired ideas about nature and culture. Again, on the sociological level, man cannot nourish his faith as before by absorbing the customs and mores which once were dispensed *en masse* by the culture or the community. Nowadays, man's faith must be nourished in the encounter with and free choice between the social, political, personal, and even religious elements in a pluralistic society; and not by a vicarious encounter with the culture of the early 1900's. This is not to say that faith in development need not be supported by tradition and history, nor that it should not turn there also for nourishment. What we are saying, however, is that man today can no longer be submissive to the past or seek in the past a present guide.

There are two important consequences of this attitude of faith, and it is essential that these consequences affect the faith of men of tomorrow.

A. FIRST CONSEQUENCE

Faith should develop, not in the manner of osmosis where man absorbs values from nature and society, but in an active manner in which man transforms this nature and this society.

In fact, man in his new state of freedom is placed in a new relationship to the world around him and to society. The new transition in his approach to life is similar to the change of roles that occur between childhood and adulthood. At the beginning of his life, he is dependent on his parents and receives everything from them. When he becomes an adult, he has a new relationship with them, not that of receiving, but of giving something of himself. He now assumes the new role of helper, the position of mother or father. And thus it should be in his life of faith. Faith must develop for the men of tomorrow not in the state of dependence on nature as much as in being able to use it. Moreover, faith cannot be developed by receiving the image of God from society; rather, faith should help make this present society more human and make it more in accord with the image of God. In other words, the new freedom of man should make him less content to acquiesce to a set order in life that is given once and for all times; rather, it should make him want to be creative. His faith will be nourished in the future less by being submissive than by making an encounter, by meeting, by remodelling the face of society.

If man in the future becomes active and creative in all that concerns his interpersonal relations and his relations and control of the earth, and if, on the other hand, in his approach to the faith, he were to remain content with the simple teaching of rote lessons, and if he thought he could have the title of faithful Christian by submitting passively to the forms and the approaches of the world and the Church without assuming responsibility for them himself, then his faith would run the great risk of dying.[3]

3. ". . . with the help of advances in psychology and in the art and science of teaching, children and young people should be assisted in the

B. SECOND CONSEQUENCE

Faith must develop in seeking the ultimate meaning of the world it is in.

Almost every aspect of today's world is new and without precedent. The development of the means of communication, the expansion of our potential for knowledge and understanding, make us somewhat uneasy. We sense that this world is becoming the only world. There is no longer a heaven out there or above; the only heaven is the fullness of earth. God is still transcendent, of course, but transcendent as Absolute Source and as an infinitely gratuitous Gift. False transcendence is that which holds God at a distance from man. The false god is he whom we imagine as a stranger and who is exterior to man.

Truth is not outside man, estranged from man, apart from him. Truth is in the direction of the totality of man. Jesus Christ did not come from heaven as a wonder-worker to make sensational revelations. Jesus Christ, Son of God, revealed in His own existence, His own being, what is the norm of mankind and the law of the world.

The recent process of demythologization and of the purifying of certain religious concepts are only the consequence of that experience which came to man as truth and which gave man a desire, —a desire to know. The way of discovering God cannot

harmonious development of their physical, moral, and intellectual endowments. Surmounting hardships with a gallant and steady heart, they should be helped to acquire gradually a more mature sense of responsibility towards ennobling their own lives through constant effort, and towards pursuing authentic freedom." *Declaration on Christian Education*, Article 1.

come except through the discovery of the total meaning of man and of man in the world. If there is a God, He can only be in the direction of the value included in the totality of man and his history.

In this view, either we will reach God in the direction of man, or man's faith will evaporate because it is not based on the reality of man with God, but on God without man. Either we will uncover God in the experience of the depths of man that includes his own grasp of the world, or his faith will be lost because it is not tied to the earth.[4]

It is here, then, that we find the true problem of faith for the young people who are coming to their place in the world. It will only be through stimulating contact with men and the world that they will develop their faith. If the present development of freedom leads our students to construct their lives on the basis of what the world presents, it is useless to look elsewhere for the framework of their faith. Their faith will not pass outside of these paths.

What precisely, therefore, is the task of the teacher? It is this: To help his students see how the ways of life in the world are sources for the life of faith. How? Essentially, it is in the measure that young people are capable of going to the depth of meaning, to the ultimate significance of human and earthly reality, that they will be able to give assent and development to their faith. The more they can truly meet reality in the

4. "In fulfilling the mandate she has received from her divine Founder to proclaim the mystery of salvation to all men, and to restore all things in Christ, holy mother Church must be concerned with the whole of man's life, even the earthly part of it insofar as that has a bearing on his heavenly calling." *Ibid.*, Introduction.

world with understanding and perception, the more they will find the God of Jesus Christ.

To exist in the faith, it is not enough to have a superficial grasp of nature or of the social and world-wide areas of involvement today. We must have a profound and real understanding of the ultimate significance of these currents and forces. That is what will distinguish the Christian in the world. He will be satisfied neither with the organizational approach for its own sake, nor with the organization which becomes more and more operative and perfect in the view of progress for man. The Christian must be as capable as every other man in the area of technique and function; he must demand, however, to know the why at all times, to see a relationship to the ultimate end of things which his richer and deeper view of things (his faith) tells him are essential.

It will be necessary for him to take care that the questions of operation and action do not become completely separate from the questions of direction and value. For the Christian, the greater action or operation will always be related to the highest meaning. To see the real meaning behind an operation, to go to the permanent value rather than the immediate, to seek the infinite value rather than the immediate temporal success, this is, it seems, the approach for the education in faith for our times.

Let us take the example of vacations in our own society. Not so very long ago a vacation was, for most men, a luxury. Now it is part of a way of life. Leisure time is not only commonplace to much of our society, but it is written into our employment. (There are exceptions, as witness the whole area of the poverty program in operation now, but for an example let us work with the problem of the leisure society.) What is the role of the vacation, of the use of leisure time in a society where the average work week allows for two days recreation, and the average work year two, three, or four weeks vacation? The question of hobbies or creative activities has become, for some, a rather abiding issue. Television ads tell us to "come on down." Life can become exciting with a week in Las Vegas. We even have magazines totally dedicated to our holidays.

For the vacationing Christian, two weeks in Cape Cod or Fort Lauderdale is not ordinarily an occasion of crisis. He will usually find his place for worship. He is not going into a new, completely different way of life. Generally, he travels and vacations in a style somewhat similar to his own life at home. The more important question concerns what he is accomplishing on vacation. Is he re-creating himself? Does he see a relationship between his life of faith and his recreation?

We ought to guide our students to see, therefore, that leisure time has other, more important purposes than the functional ones of relaxation, enjoyment, the playing of games. It will be incumbent on us to educate our students to see that such functions must be dependent on the deeper meaning and the real idea of leisure. A man takes his vacation as a Christian only if he asks himself at the beginning what is the whole meaning, the divine meaning of leisure, recreation, vacation in human and social life. He must consciously make his recreational plans and take his vacation in view of the utlimate meaning of his need for rest and relaxation as a human being. Whoever will make such a profound rethinking and redirection in his faith will never cease to meet the Lord in all the persons he meets and the things he does. This may sound strange to our ears, but perhaps it is because we are not accustomed to thinking of the Lord in our total life. The Lord is present to us in all our human relationships. We must try to be present to Him by our total existence.

2. POSSIBLE APPROACHES

In view of what we have said, the questions which arise from the catechetical point of view are the following: How can we both transmit the Church's teachings on dogma and morals, which are not to be invented by the students, and at the same time inculcate in him a personal faith that he must unceasingly recreate and invent under the impulse of the Holy Spirit? How does one present the letter of the law in such a manner that it leads to the Spirit and makes the student capable of recreating his own personal "letter" or approach within the framework of dogma and morals? How can one present revelation in such a way that it will be developed, utilized personally, and deepened gradually by the student in every new situation?

We offer here three suggestions which may give insight into this problem.

1. We Must Lead Our Students to Acquire Personal Principles of Doctrine

Kaufmann and Cathelin have written of the conditions for a renewal of teaching: "The aim of pedagogy is the transmission of a certain number of elements of appreciation. These must enable the students to constitute for themselves a personal basis or personal means of investigation and grasp of and on the world. A pedagogy of metallic framework that would replace a pedagogy of a solid-wall type . . . We must exact from the students a personal adjustment to the conditions of reality. All choices must be exercised in a structural perspective; this is the major problem, for the student as well as for the teacher. In a post-Einsteinian universe, the new pedagogy must train students to grasp, as they happen, the processes of relationships, the events acting on other events, and which thus give the final significance of what is happening; and this goes beyond verbal definitions and varied Scholastic dictates of history or tradition."[5]

What significance can Kaufmann and Cathelin's phrase, giving a certain number of "elements of appreciation," have in religious education? We have already used this phrase in other words in "principles of doctrine" which prepare the students to construct a life of faith. Therefore, does this not also mean to give the students a metallic framework around which they could construct their life of faith, and not as in the past a wall which we as teachers have already and definitively constructed for them?

By personal principles of doctrine we mean doctrinal principles which have been elaborated personally by the individual, propositions which make the link between historical revelation and living experience; in other words, what is to be brought about is an understanding of the Christian message not of itself alone, but in relation to life and in relation to its meaning in the world. So the historical fact of Abraham will not be received as something of itself; but in the concrete understanding of the word of God, a man today will read this event in salvation history as

5. *Le gaspillage de la liberté,* Paris, 1964, p. 180.

more than a historical fact. In connection with the many things in his own life, with the many experiences proper to himself, he will strive to grasp the full meaning of this event of grace in his life.

Joining the Abraham event to his own life and receiving insight from it, contemporary man can apply to his own situation some basic principles and "elements of appreciation" in the following style: All great things depend on faith; faith is not an absurdity, but a very deep understanding of events and laws of life. Whoever believes runs the risk of a very demanding life, but he will be a creator of life through it; the spirit always triumphs.

Thus stated, these principles could still seem abstract. Yet we should not be mistaken on this matter, for what characterizes these "elements of appreciation" is that they have been discovered in a kind of constant to-and-fro movement between actual life and historical revelation. Because this is so, they are not dead letters, but active principles. Or, if you prefer, they are viewpoints which constantly bring a student into contact with life, forcing him to interpret, to be creative. This is not a hidden talent, but an active talent which does not cease to develop itself precisely because it is part of him. A student will not learn it by repetition, but by his own creation from his own experience. That principle must come to him as spirit, not letter only, for the very manner in which it is transmitted makes it necessary for him to recreate it in himself, to seize the points of vital application in order to understand it. Abraham becomes meaningful to him because the student has brought him into his own life. He has seen what was true in Abraham and for himself.

It would be perfectly vain and sterile to busy ourselves here over the question of whether our teaching should start from the point of historic revelation or, on the other side, from life now. The starting point is not important; what is essential is to link up, to unite, to come to an element of doctrine that is personally understood by the student as having a relationship to him and his life. And this can be done in three ways.

1. It is necessary, in the first place, always to make the connection between salvation history and life, always to know the implications in real life that are found in salvation history, and vice versa. So we can never be satisfied in our teaching with either a doctrinal formula in itself or a purely human outlook on life.

2. It is also necessary to have this relationship discovered by the student himself. We must never do it for him. There can be principles of doctrine that he refers to only when he has started to discover for himself the relationship between revelation and life. On the one hand, a student's discovery will have an objective content since it includes a grasp of the word of God. On the other hand, this discovery, this personal re-creation, is the assurance that discovery and exploration will continue later in life. He is here developing the habit of discovery, of invention, of adapting himself.

3. It is necessary, finally, that the relationship between the message of God and life have a realistic character. The danger will be that our students will build in a purely notional or idealistic manner, somewhat similar to that produced when the religious education is given in a "cloistered" style, unrelated to the real world outside. On the contrary, the adolescent must be led to a realistic relationship between the message of Christ and the world which really exists, a world which the student will come to know more and more as he grows.

2. We Must Lead Our Students to Be Responsible for Their Education in Faith

Should we allow our students to choose for themselves the subject areas to be covered, either for periods of time or for the year?

This question has often been posed to teachers. And every teacher whose "yes" to the question was prompted only by his concern to develop the interests that his students already have, runs the risk of abandoning objective values to the students' subjective needs. Yet we must also keep in mind that it is necessary to take into consideration not only the object learned, but also the subject learning. For ourselves, we are still conscious that we must consider the interests of youth and the demands of life in the Church. What, we must ask ourselves, do our principles of freedom mean in terms of developing freedom in the faith with our students?

At the beginning of the school year the juniors or seniors may propose the following for their course in religious education: sex, the nature of woman, the principles of Communism, civil rights, the rights of conscience. This may seem to be very far from a syllabus which allows us to teach Christ and His Church.

The above program would definitely be far removed from the one listed in the syllabus if these particular students had not been previously educated to a true freedom in the faith, if they had not had the occasion during the course of their development to become responsible in their own growth and maturing in the faith. In that case, in fact, the students' discussions and exchanges on the subjects they want, while perhaps valuable in themselves, would unfold in a superficial manner and only touch on partial aspects of the total reality.

But let us take the other possibility. These same topics, requested by students who are sensitive to what appeals to their own age and who have been trained in freedom, are what are needed at this point in their life. At each step in growth, these students have been drawn to go beyond the immediate plans, views, and values which they have previously accepted. They know it is possible to go beyond the particular point and to search for the ultimate meaning, and that from partial aspects they can proceed to the truth which is coherent and complete. They have, moreover, little by little acquired a certain responsibility for their education in the faith. They feel concerned by everything that touches on their life because it touches on their faith.

Now then, proceeding from the subjects which they themselves have chosen, will it be so difficult to develop these themes into a program? Leading his students by questions and suggestions, will it be so difficult for the teacher to unfold such aspects of the truth about which the students have never dreamed? Or better yet, could he not proceed from actual events, in order to help his students to be attentive to the total picture of the reality they have asked to be discussed? Lastly, the teacher could bring into his students' program by careful use of insights, references, and perspectives, the points to be covered by the official syllabus which are implicitly in the students' suggestions?

What is the difference in this approach? It is this: In place of imposing by authority on the students a list of preconceived materials to be covered, we help them develop the program, but one which flows from their interests, their lives, their situations, and try to help them unravel all that is really involved in their existence. The program of study is not abandoned; it is made progressively more pertinent. It has become a need for the student.

In sum, it is necessary for us to see that at the age of sixteen to eighteen, the adolescent, who has become capable of discerning his own needs in religious education, can himself decide on his course of study; that is to say, he ought to be able to choose the topics he wants to learn about. This means, in other words, that he can decide on the ways in which he will search into and make more profound his own faith. The teacher will not be a master who imposes, but a witness to the Church, a witness who will help his advance, help deepen his search, and guide him in truth.

Therefore, the student will come to resolve his religious problems, we believe, not by being presented with an abstract discussion of the questions of the subject at hand, but by being given and encouraged in freedom and responsibility to work out for himself—under the guidance of his teacher—the answers to the problem as it affects him. As educators, we are to educate to freedom in the faith. This is, perhaps, to give up some of our own responsibility so that our students may themselves become more responsible.

3. We Must Lead Our Students to Be Inventive in Their Life of Faith

It is less a question here of a strictly catechetical approach, and more one of an educational insight. It is necessary to develop in the adolescent the ability and the habit to create and not only to repeat learned lessons, to ask questions and not only to take notes in class, to refer intelligently to the Christian community and the authority of Christ and not only to live in passive conformity with that authority, expecting from it directions and instructions. In other words, we are to give our students the taste for and the habit of directing themselves, in full freedom, towards an unceasingly profound growth in the faith and in personal decisions which are not preformed by others.

The teacher will have to be careful, therefore, that he does not, more or less consciously, make the students depend on him as the master. Conscious of the process of identification, the influence of the group itself, idealization, all of which are characteristic of evolution throughout adolescence, the teacher must guide his students towards a greater development of freedom. More particularly, along the lines already pointed out by Carl Rogers,[6] the teacher should be able to accept times of incoherence and disorder, even moments of anxiety, which are necessary in order that the adolescent may free himself of his need for a paternal image. The teacher must learn to accept little by little, not to reassure the student by appreciation or disapprobation, but to let the adolescent form his own judgment by himself, to shape his own appreciation of himself.

No doubt, this involves a total rethinking and renewal of attitudes in teaching. Formerly, having given our approval to or even adopted certain authoritarian and paternal approaches in our teaching, it is certain that we stilled in our students their power of invention. As a result, we ended up with students who were safe and sure in their faith, individuals who could live the mechanical or rote aspects of their faith; but we did not bring

6. In *Counseling and Psychotherapy,* New York, 1942.

forth the creators, the inventors, students who searched for themselves.

4. We Must Lead Our Students to Go Beyond the Surface of Things

Young people are spontaneously drawn by questions of how to do something: how to pass an examination, how to make friends, how to be successful. It is characteristic of their age, part of the way things are.

The real art of religious education, in our time, consists in placing these functional, practical questions in the greater perspective, that of the significance, the meaning of action, and the ultimate end and purpose of things. In other words, all the art—and when we fail, all the anguish—of religious education consists in posing the ultimate questions. In a certain fashion, we have here the idea of Teilhard de Chardin: if the intellectuals are without religion, without faith, it is because their vision has not gone to the root of things; they have established laws, given us observations and facts of nature, but they have not dared to be as strong in posing the problem of meaning and of the ultimate directions.

But how do we go about posing questions that go to the root of things? How do we make students dissatisfied with the superficial grasp of the world and make them go beyond to the ultimate meaning? Such is our problem in religious education. It is the eternal question which is always present in the faith, but one made more demanding in our time by the appeal of the world to our students, an appeal which could lead them to a surface understanding only when they need a true appreciation and deep understanding of the reality of the world.

A. IN ORDER TO UNSETTLE OUR STUDENTS' COMPLACENCIES ABOUT VALUES ACCEPTED UNQUESTIONINGLY

The role of the teacher is to be one who unsettles, who provokes thoughts, who disturbs complacency. He should be one who, because he sees the root of things, the object of the world and of being, demands that his students not stop at the surface and the periphery of reality. This will be evident in the way he asks questions, in the manner in which he places in view the paradoxes involved in certain assumed positions, certain facile truths.

One is not truly an educator because one finishes the material and is content to furnish solutions to problems raised by the students. The true teacher will be the one who, anxious above all about the quality of searching and questioning, will want to raise the most searching questions, those which put into the thinking of the students questions about the ultimate end of the earth, the eternity of love, the fullness of life. Students have suffered too long from teachers of religion who have the answers for everything. Perhaps it is more important to have teachers who, in the manner of Job and Abraham, pose questions to God and to the earth.

B. IN ORDER TO UNFOLD TO OUR STUDENTS THE POSSIBILITIES ABOUT THE ULTIMATE MEANINGS OF THINGS

How do we propose to direct our students towards the ultimate meaning, the true dimensions of things, if they do not have the taste for it and will not open themselves to its attraction?

There exists, actually, a correspondence and a secret connection between the things that call for expression in the adolescent and the actual reality which he has not yet uncovered. More exactly, if he feels the call of certain things, it is a sign that he is already drawn into these things and their mystery; their true meaning is within him like a seed.

We believe, then, that young people want to go to the depths of things and that they want to do so because they have an unforced attraction towards what is greatest and best.

To help them go to the ultimate dimensions of reality, therefore, means that the teacher must detect the possibilities in his students, listen to their desires and hopes, and at the same time infinitely to respect all the possibilities within them. Yet even more, the teacher must have in his contact with them—that is, while proceeding from the concrete questions they pose—a very great faith in what they can become. The teacher must never fear to affirm with conviction, to be open to what is and will be, to battle and to struggle for a greatness in man which goes beyond all things to the divine.

We propose in the following some concrete suggestions and methods which may help us to achieve such a program.

3. METHODS

1. A Method Leading Towards Personal Discovery and Invention

We must help our students, through active research and group discussion, to discover for themselves and personally formulate for themselves the basic doctrinal elements of their faith.

Let us take an example. A teacher puts together and prepares an excellent catechesis on work, with a very well-planned educational approach which leads the group to think about work in the same way that the teacher does. Now let us even suppose that the theology which inspired the teacher was that of a theologian who sees work in its creative aspect. At this point we could ask whether this is the way this particular class feels about work and the way the students have experienced work.

If so, the assimilation should undoubtedly be very good, and there will be at this time a certain capacity on the part of the students for putting into practice various ideas about work which they have learned. But, we might well ask, will the teacher have succeeded in educating his students to a faith capable of discovering and adapting itself in other experiences which will occur tomorrow? We do not think so, for his students will not have searched, discovered, invented. They will have done nothing but receive from a very interesting presentation, but a presentation not sufficiently capable of stimulating their freedom. They will then have been enclosed in a doctrine, rather than having come to the doctrine itself.

But if adolescents do not experience work as creative and valuable, then what is the result of such a catechesis on work? It will be viewed as a fine doctrine, even an excellent synthesis on work; but this synthesis will be a dead letter. It will be a treasure bound to be put away, useless, precisely because it has no living meaning.

Let us imagine another teacher coming to the group who, instead of proposing a doctrine, begins by proposing a certain number of areas for research and discussion.

Example. What effect does work have on people around you? What happens to people who can no longer work? What happens to people in an area where work is not highly or properly developed, where the working conditions are not carefully thought out?

First step. Serious research should begin from the questions proposed, which the students write down. From the facts they find, they can become sensitive to the whole problem, can acquire their first real knowledge on the subject. Finally, the group may find itself drawn into an area for common research.

Second step. The next help is the opinions, the witness, the personal approach given by Christians involved in this area. The objective here is not to discover God's point of view and to define the Christian position on the subject. Again that would be the easy solution. This step in the process is directed first of all, through the contact with live positions, to stimulate the thinking of the group. It is to lead the group to discuss, to make an idea for itself in the face of the differing opinions and ideas that have been uncovered.

It is in this approach that we can ask the group to undertake interviews with Christian adults, asking such questions as why they work, or whether the Gospel offers them any insight in their work, and so forth. On all these points the teacher could be consulted and could bring his own testimony and insight, —not his own theory on work, but rather the way in which he himself considers his work in terms of the faith.

Third step. The students are led to involve themselves in more formal research on an objective formulation of the meaning of work. "Now that you have absorbed the ideas on work from people who may or may not see work in a Christian light, try

112

to discover the thought of Christ and the Church." The teacher can now proceed in two ways: he can have his students investigate scriptural texts; or he can have some type of communication on the subject with the group.

Fourth step. The students should at this point have acquired some elements of doctrinal appreciation, that is, principles which, consciously referred to revelation and the experience uncovered, will give them ways of seeing, of being, of having a grasp on the world. This is the heart of the matter. We can ask the students: From what you have learned from the witness of Christians, from what you have received from the word of God, has your idea of work changed? What new meaning has revelation given you about work?

It is by answering these and similar questions that our students will come to acquire what we have called personal principles or active principles of doctrinal reference. These are principles which are at once personal because discovered and lived by the students, and doctrinal because explicitly referred to the history of salvation.[7]

The essential element of this method is a logical development in which the students come face to face with a problem and gain an insight into the problem by an encounter with revelation and life. The resulting doctrinal propositions thus necessarily include personal experience and revelation, and they avoid any overtone of doctrinal rigidity because they have not been gained by rote learning and repetitious teaching.

7. It is possible, of course, that such an approach could be incomplete. Yet it is not wrong to bring in more formal elements according to the capacities of the group. However, the teacher must learn to judge not only the capabilities, but also the limitations, of the students with whom he is working.

It cannot be said, however, that such a method removes all the authority of the Church and of revelation. The teacher, through his own witness and contribution in raising questions, and his comments and suggestions which strengthen or correct, provides a guide to doctrinal objectivity and guarantees the truth of the doctrinal propositions which the students have discovered.

2. A Method Leading Towards Active Assimilation

Especially with early adolescents, the method of personal invention and discovery cannot always be applied. It would be, in the long run, tiring and anti-psychological in terms of their readiness, because it would not provide them with enough breathing time, for their age demands that they dream and let their imagination work free from all practical application.

That is why, with this group, we often use less exacting methods which form a transition between the class teacher-centered approach and a more inventive-discovery kind of approach.

By method of active assimilation, or active presentation, we mean a method which requires the student to take an active position before each doctrinal proposition which is presented to him. Thus, in a more formally presented program, the student is forced by a series of questions and activities to think, or more exactly to understand what is said, by constantly applying these truths to his life. For example, the teacher might ask his students, "How would you explain this part of God's message to your friends who don't believe in God? How does this message change your friendship, your reading, your work?"

The clue here is to have the students accept as understood only that which can be rethought and expressed in another way for the life they are living.

The group should often be granted moments of silence in order to make the necessary reflection on the matter at hand, and also moments of group discussion or research in order to put the message of Christ into the real situations of their life. Along the same lines, the teacher should never stop developing with the group the art of asking questions and of learning how to criticize soundly. The freedom of a group can be evaluated through the number and quality of the questions asked. There is no better reward for a teacher than a group which asks real questions, questions which have to do with life.[8]

3. On Introducing Our Students to the Tools and Methods of Learning

We have seen that it is no longer possible—if indeed it was ever possible—to know every important thing about one's life in faith; no longer possible to decide beforehand, categorically, the lines of conduct which one will follow throughout his life. And since this is so, a compact and definite collection of religious beliefs is no longer sufficient, and it becomes more and more important to substitute for the collection of belief a habit of knowing how to learn. Consequently, the educator will find it essential to his task to introduce young people to the tools and documents necessary for the continued growth of their faith.

8. This aspect is developed more completely in our work *Methodology* (New York and London, 1967).

This introduction can be developed in the students by guiding them:

—to learn to nourish their faith in dialogue;

—to receive and interpret in faith the documents which come from authority; to discover and discern their worth; to know where to find them;

—to develop a sound critical judgment of religious reports given in the newspapers, magazines, on radio and TV;

—to read the published materials on the faith, the biblical and theological journals, magazines of current Catholic interest, special reports and lectures.

What is important here is to emphasize the spirit which should give life to our religious education and formation if we are to educate Christians capable of responsibility and development in today's world, if we are to bring forth Christians capable of a freedom which expresses itself in faith.

This is the very heart of religious education in our time: to help our students to understand the need for a permanent basis for their faith, and to give them a desire for and the means to acquire such a basis; but also to prepare them always to learn more about their faith, to absorb, rethink, and adapt to a changing world of which their faith is a part.

For psycho-sociological reasons, it is still necessary to maintain that one of the aims of the religious education of young children is to lead them to acquire a general and objective knowledge about their faith. But the ultimate aim of the religious education of adolescents is to instill in them the habit of exercising their personal principles of doctrine, principles which our students can always refer to and expand in this changing world and Church of our time.

4. REFLECTIONS

1. Are we ready to present the message of Christ essentially as a message which we have known through our own profound understanding of the world?

2. If we learn to discover, it is frequently because we have been with one person who has taught us the excitement of uncovering, of searching, of finding. Can our students learn, through us, that they must constantly rethink and rediscover their faith and their life in a world that is always in change? Do we give them the witness of adaptability?

3. Can a teacher, convinced of the importance of educating in freedom in the faith, evade the problem which disturbs the consciences of adolescents—the religious constraints imposed by institutions, organizations, societies? Does the institution take precedence over dialogue or dogma?

4. A discovery of personal principles of doctrine demands much patience, truth, humility on the part of the teacher. Have we deliberately chosen to lead our students slowly to freedom, or are we rushing them by way of memorization and stereotyped answers and solutions?

V.

COMMITMENT
TO THE WORLD

Religious education will strive to educate the young people of today to Christian action and behavior which is committed to and in the service of the world.[1]

1. POSSIBLE APPROACHES

In this section, three phases of religious education will be considered: education to action, to behavior, and to involvement in and to the service of today's world.

1. Educating to Action

First of all, religious programs must educate to action. This is a well-known theme. A religious program that does not lead to action is like a dead letter.

1. "Moreover, they should be trained to take their part in social life, so that by proper instruction in necessary and useful skills they can become actively involved in various community organizations, be ready for dialogue with others, and be willing to act energetically on behalf of the common good." *Declaration on Christian Education,* Article 1.

A. WHAT ACTION?

Everybody talks of action, but precisely what is meant by the term? Is action participating in some specific form of the apostolate, in some definite parish activity? If we wish to comprehend the place of action in religious education and to discover the true educational methods needed in order to stimulate our students to real Christian actions, we can hardly be content with such paltry definitions.

By action, we mean the commitment of the whole person to a cause, —"synthesis of will, knowledge, and being," says Blondel. It is not a question of such and such a practical action, defined in advance—which would easily be an evasion of a real action, a source of illusion and of a good conscience—but a commitment of the person expressing in his whole being what is understood and grasped by his intelligence, and, if by a believer, in his thinking enlightened by faith.

Of course, we have to be careful not to fool ourselves. The young person, the adolescent especially, is little prepared for real action in the sense of commitment to the world. His life is still in its becoming stage; he is in development and growth. He is involved more in projects than in reality. How can we dare ask him, therefore, for a profound, decisive commitment to action?[2]

2. The problem of educating teenagers and young people to action is a very complex one. Because we are not dealing with adults, the objective requirements of an apostolic engagement in a specific environment, or a specific world, need always be subordinated, it seems, to the subjective requirements of temperament, internal maturity. Otherwise we force nature.

Yet we must be careful not to go too far in minimizing his capabilities or potential. For inasmuch as a teenager becomes conscious of his own personality, he begins to put it into action, that is, he begins to pledge it, to commit it somewhat. Will he have the chance of meeting, at that moment, a teacher who is sensitive enough to open the adolescent to the vast horizons of the action of Christ in the world, a teacher who will see to it that the teenager's progressing psychological development is noticed and strengthened, challenged and developed within natural limits? This is, it seems to us, the real way to approach the problem that the teacher of religion faces in educating to action.[3]

B. HOW CAN RELIGIOUS EDUCATION DEVELOP A SENSE OF ACTION IN THE ADOLESCENT?

In accordance with the psychology of adolescents and the principles of religious psychology, we answer this question mainly in one word: we must educate the student to action by "calling" him.[4] To speak to him by way of calling him is the most effective way in which we can educate him to action.

3. It is certain that education to action can and must be seen from different angles, as that of Catholic Action for example. For here, in educating to action, the teacher will refer much more to the needs of the environment. Education in this case will make much more use of revision and project than calling and teaching. The two forms are complementary.

4. No doubt, there are other ways of proceeding: we insist here on one which appears to us as major and specific, leaving aside many other conditions described elsewhere: a need for a twentieth-century language, for a reflection on daily happenings, for a study of world structures and the environmental situations, for an educator who recognizes values and is also a man of action; and finally, the need for a catechetical style where teaching, education, and experience are intimately linked.

What, then, does the term "calling" mean?

Educating to action, in religious education, is not telling students, "You have to commit yourself to something," although at times it may be necessary to exert some pressure on them to begin to act. Rather, educating to action is mainly teaching our students in such a way that we show the greatness, the seriousness, the value of the tasks waiting for them. It is to show them how Christ calls to them within the poor, the sick, in this and that dehumanizing structure or unjust situation. It is suffering with those who suffer, being deeply committed when talking of God, and being possessed by the infinite generosity of the Lord to "do something."

Educating to action is talking of the Eucharist, grace, hell, and all parts of the message in relation to the practical needs of man. It is never talking abstractly of revelation, but always making it a part of temporal reality. If the teacher speaks of the sacrament of the Eucharist only to define it in remote terms of a "mode or presence of Christ in the soul," there are few chances that his teaching will lead his students to action. It will remain in the air, an ideal with little life, little "call." But if sacramental communion is presented as the progressive invasion of the great love of Jesus Christ purifying and making infinite the chaos and confusion of our human loves, of our mutterings of prayer, then suddenly the students listen. They somehow sense that they are being called to a great life, and that consequently it is important to communicate in the body and blood of Christ. They realize that to be alive, they must transform their small ways of loving and enlarge their love by opening to others.

C. THE CONDITIONS FOR AN EDUCATION THAT "CALLS"

The term "calling" needs to be considered more precisely because it is one of the keys to the religious education of adolescents, who by definition are at a stage of vocation, of calling, an age of becoming. What are the conditions required for an education of "calling"?

To call someone is first of all *to discern in him his unique possibilities*. It is to discover the privileged way by which he is great, unique, and original. The first approach of understanding the vocation, the calling, in another is this discernment and this discovery of possibilities.

What we mean is that in religious education, the message should never be given out of context and setting, abruptly or illogically, but must always be directed to given needs and possibilities. Since the teacher is to announce the good news, he should first learn to listen to and believe in his hearers. Only a teacher who first believes in his students can call them. And we should keep this fact in mind when we begin our encounters with our students in their religious education. Our catechesis must never be obvious or heavy-handed, our encounter never such that the students are thereby put ill at ease; yet we must never compromise in setting careful guidelines for our students, taking care in every situation to respect and appreciate the value of each person in our group.

To call our students is to address them in such a way that their own possibilities are stirred, brought to life. It is to present the good news to them in such a way that they come to see the connection between their human possibilities and the Gospel call to fullness.

122

Let us take the example of grace. If we present it in much the same way as we would describe an electric power station, with the current cut off by sin, we are describing an objective reality which does not personally concern or reach the adolescent's sense of himself. If we speak of it as a personal act, however, infinitely positive and valuable, by which God stimulates the student's need for life and goodness in order to enter a full existence, then we reach the adolescent and develop his possibilities for relying on the gift of God.

For us to call our students is to affirm our belief in their beginnings and their potential for growth. It is to ask them to take the first step and believe in their own potential. In religious teaching, this means to announce a God who is with them, who has dialogued with man all through history, who accompanies man through all the stages of human development to assure and stimulate and correct him. He is a God who is sensitive to the ordeal but also joy of adolescence, and who is truly present to them as they grow.

Finally, to call our students is to entrust them with a task with which they can test their strength, their yearnings, their desires. In our catechesis this means that the word must provoke commitment from them, in a general way in that we propose examples of how our students could commit themselves in a Christian way to this or that cause in the Church or the world, and thereby engender in them a spirit of commitment; and perhaps also in a more specific way in that we propose various actvities in which our students can realize their spirit of commitment in a tangible way.[5]

5. Following times and place, and according to the themes studied in a particular religious program, the teacher is expected to propose different

2. *Educating to Behavior*

If teenagers were asked what they most wanted in their education, they would perhaps say that they want to know how to "act in front of people." Anxious, awkward, timid, flamboyant, they experiment in social behavior, on how to give the desired image of themselves, on how to conduct themselves with a show of finesse, on how to get along; in short, on how to succeed in the world as though they weren't really trying. This is a major adolescent preoccupation.

It is a rather sad paradox, therefore, when many young people, especially those coming out of parochial and diocesan schools, complain of not being prepared to live in the world once they have graduated. They say, "We have been taught about things which have no connection with what's going on. All we have is a lot of impractical ideals to go by." They are, in a sense, students who have studied the map of medieval Christendom for four or eight or twelve years, and who are then sent into the United States to live.

We have to provide our students with a real map, a map of the United States, of Europe, Asia, Africa. This is where they live, it is their season. It is not enough to tell them, say, "Love your neighbor," and then send them out of the school door. We have

---

commitments along the hierarchical line which the Church herself establishes. Those apostolic activities most closely related to the existing structures in the Church—for example, the CCD—cannot be presented as only one example among many others. There must be a question of values in different work and an understanding of the capabilities and maturity of the students.

to help them learn first of all what it means to love, and also who their neighbor is, and where they can find him.

We must also help our students learn how to react to the realities around them. We are to teach young people the secrets of a human and Christian behavior in an apartment house or while on vacation, teach them how to have a normal boy-girl relationship, how to read a newspaper with judgment, how to analyze advertisements. Adolescents are not to be handed ready-made solutions; rather, we are to teach them to observe, to analyze new situations, to judge, to search for the material below the surface, to know where to find needed information, and finally to take a definite position on issues with humility. Teen-agers must become capable of practical judgments and worthy decisions, and not only learn theoretical, abstract moral laws.

Gaston Berger insists on the necessity of educating students by way of select information and choice. "Nobody can now 'know everything' any more," he writes, "have read everything, have understood everything. Moreover, we have come to doubt the usefulness of this approach; and if the quantity of new information is to become, during a lifetime, superior to man's past acquisition of knowledge, then the necessity of knowing how to make choices necessarily precludes the alternative of knowing much. . . . Learning how to find a specific reference that one needs may be the new principal aim of teaching."[6]

It seems to us that such is the best direction for us to take in educating our students in how to behave. And this supposes that we give new accents to our programs and methods in religious teaching: less religious culture, less abstract discussions, less hand-

6. In *Prospectives,* October, 1961.

ing out of principles; more constant concern to have our students find solutions by themselves, proceeding from real and concrete problems, formulating a catechesis centered more on adaptation to life than on cultural refinement, a catechesis which has as its aim and model a quality-filled group life rather than "a perfect teacher."

Perhaps this will involve much practical work and information which will not be strictly catechetical, such as furnishing our students with objective information on public relations. But God has not called us to be catechists in order that we may be loyal to theoretical definitions. Rather, He has called us to live more abundantly and in the world that exists.[7]

A last reason which brings us to decide for this education of behavior: Jesus Christ has become too much of a stranger to the world for a Christian to live in this world without concern, without a need to be a witness to or sign of the Lord. What the Christian says, does, or writes must always be concerned with reaching the non-Christian, the de-Christianized.[8] The Church since Vatican II can no longer be defined as a juridical society, as an untouchable house at the summit of a mountain. Now we must think of it as a sign among nations, as the sacrament of Christ in human life. Youth must be educated in such a way that

7. Certain books concerned about religious education show a great concern for such adaptation. In the series *Complete Group Guidance for Catholic High Schools,* for instance, we find the following chapter headings: "You and Your School"—"How to Conduct a School Meeting"— "How to Present Yourself for a Job"—"Personality Analysis"—"Why You Should Worry About Your Career"—"The Will of God: A Rule of Life"— "Hypocritical Attitudes in Everyday Life"—"How to Explain the Catholic Faith to Others."

8. See Rahner, *The Christian Commitment,* pp. 23–27.

126

they will want to be signs whose behavior has something to say to the world of today. They cannot default from this task, evade it, or absent themselves from it altogether. For such is the way of the Holy Spirit in our time

3. Educating to Commitment and Service

Action alone is not the answer. One can be very active and still not be committed to reality. Nor is behavior alone the solution. One can react in a manner that is adapted to the world today without ever taking any action. For it is still necessary that our active presence be involved, be commited to and in the service of the world.

What do we mean by commitment?

Perhaps this comparison will help us. A car comes off a small country road or city street and gets on to a super-highway which carries bumper-to-bumper traffic. The car is now part of the whole stream of traffic and must be alert to the possibility of sudden stops in front of it and the reaction of the driver behind. If the driver of the car can and does decide to get out of this traffic, he removes himself from a commitment to drive at a certain speed, with certain cautions dictated by the particular situation. Does this exiting change his basic driving? No, but he is no longer committed to a certain pattern: he has disengaged himself.

Now, it is our task to educate our students to commitment, to engagements. We are to help them place themselves in the real situations which are around them, and have them measure and evaluate these situations. Too frequently, adolescents get into situations where they satisfy themselves with a certain fervor, even a certain action, but under their own terms, not the terms of the real situation. Have we prepared them for a true encounter with the world as it is and under the conditions the world may be in? Have they learned to accept the delays, the slow movement of conversions, the stop-and-go of the human march? Our privilege is to educate, to lead them fully to the Christian commitment with all its difficulties, involvements, and delays. Religious training cannot ignore the essential aspect of life as it is. It must educate our students to engage themselves. At times, it may seem easier to choose some privileged forms of action which are very worthy in themselves but which are really removed from the reality that demands our students' involvement, their giving of themselves with others in a commitment to the world.

We must never cease to stimulate the faith of our students with involvement and commitment. How does the Eucharist become a part of their own milieu, culture, neighborhood? How they live the Eucharist, not only in their personal relations, but in the context of the school cafeteria where each one of them is seeking the quickest and best service for himself? How can one begin to communicate with others in such a situation?

What is important here is that their religious education begin not only with the psychological situation or a particular incident, but that its emphasis be on the situation that reflects the structures of the world today.[9]

9. We do not mean to imply, naturally, that environmental structures are the only important ones. More and more are other structures coming to have a major shaping influence on young people: such as places of recreation, vacation spots, newspapers, school clubs, all interpersonal exchanges and dialogues.

2. REFLECTIONS

1. Can we notice at the end of a meeting with our students that they have the desire to act on or change their way of being; or have they left the meeting saying merely that what we have to say was "interesting"?

2. When we present a particular idea to our students, do we really consider the possibilities for living these ideas? Do we give them examples, some practical insights, some personal view, some points that can be put into practice rather immediately?

3. In providing our students with moral guides, do we go about it by setting up for them various theoretical moral principles, and enjoin them to "apply" these principles; or do we attempt to arouse them to exercise their conscience in the everyday situations which they encounter in the world?

4. Have we gone into problems relating to the Christian transformation of culture and society, and of the Church; or have we stopped short at the psychological level, at individual problems of limited scope?

VI.

THE GROUP APPROACH

Our aim in religious education will not be concentrated on the individual so much as on the group and interpersonal relations. This group education supposes less of the presence of the teacher as the sole authority but more of his presence as guide in a fraternal relation; his will be less a direct and authoritative action than an action or direction aimed at stirring up the group's own initiatives and at helping to develop its members.

1. THE IMPORTANCE AND NEWNESS OF THIS APPROACH

We are dealing here with an essentially pedagogical suggestion or direction. We use the words "direction or suggestion" to indicate that we are not condemning all past approaches or completely eliminating all other ideas in favor of this approach. What we suggest here is an approach which in many respects is relatively new in the religious education of adolescents.

Although there has been in this country a long-established interest in and research on the methods and scope of group education, there is nevertheless still a need for more detailed and stricter analysis and understanding of its techniques. The suggestions which follow, however, are made primarily for the purpose of investigating possible new approaches in and attitudes towards group education.[1]

2. THE ELEMENTS OF THIS APPROACH

Group education contains two elements which are inter-related: (1) the development of the group situation as an educational tool; (2) a new presence of the teacher, a new role in relation to the group.

1. First Element: The Development of the Group Situation

The question here is not so much of educating individuals as individuals, as of educating all of the students in terms of the group and in terms of interpersonal relationships.

A. INTERPERSONAL RELATIONSHIPS

Educators occasionally complain, "Adolescents live only in groups; they have no distinctive personality." However, such educators perhaps fail to see that the group does not abolish or diminish the personalities of its members, but gives them a new definition, a new characteristic.

Formerly, it was said of one that he had personality if it was quite apparent that he could "get along by himself," if his princi-

1. In our book *Methodology* we take up in greater detail a number of the techniques of group education.

ples and habits were uniquely his own, if he shared in what Herbert Hoover called "the American system of rugged individualism."[2] Nowadays, however, a new definition of personality is in the ascendancy, given less in terms of the individual's internal make-up and more in terms of his relationship with others. In this definition, then, having personality is being capable of sustaining profound and varied personal relations, being as much capable of being influenced by human groups as influencing them, being capable of making decisions which have not one's own good as the motive, but the good of the group.

B. TYPE OF LEADERSHIP

The key to group leadership is not in a "big shot," not in one who "has it made" in one way or another, but in one who is responsible, who is capable of giving life to the group. The leader of the group can no longer be some "solitary" figure who almost by his silence and isolation establishes the mores and direction of the group; rather, it must today be someone who walks with the group, and is like the other members of the group. He is essentially someone who, in the group, has enough insight to draw back to analyze a situation and to discover its possibilities. He has enough authority to present his analysis of a situation to the group and to stimulate a response to the necessary choices to be made. He possesses enough competence to ask questions and to conduct a democratic meeting on a problem. He is a catalyst who can bring about dialogue. He initiates action and encourages responsibility.

2. In a campaign speech of October 22, 1928, in New York.

C. THE FORMATION OF GROUPS

As adolescents become conscious of interpersonal relationships, it is important not to push them into large groupings, to expect them to express themselves in the larger, more structured societies. More than is the case with any other group, adolescents need smaller groups, groups in which they feel recognized, supported, and stimulated. Without this basic group experience, they will never be prepared for the more objective and demanding social processes which adult life will require of them.

Today, more than ever, it is of the greatest importance that the teacher direct his attention to the creation of the viable group; or, if the group already exists, he must direct his attention to its particular spirit and quality. Before being concerned about the program to be taught, before being preoccupied with the students' interest in the course, the teacher must ask himself at the beginning of the school year about the quality and the spirit of the students as a group. In a class where students are artificially gathered together, he must seek to make this assembly of individuals conscious of their relations to one another and of their responsibilities to one another. He must ask himself: Does this class have any sense of being a group, of having a meaning as a group? Does each person in the group have a regard for every other person? Are all the members of the group open to expressing themselves? Are they aware of the contributions they can make?

Each time the students come together as a true group, the teacher should see to it that the message, instead of being an instruction imposed on the students from outside, becomes something that is alive to the whole group, something that incites questions and thought for them all. The teacher will have to help them look into the message and also help each one to express it himself.

The teacher will, little by little, lead all in the group to express themselves, watching that no one hides unnecessarily behind the wall of timidity or fear. Each person, by his own call, has a unique word to say that no one else can say. It falls to the teacher to help each student to become responsible, not only for speaking, but also for asking questions, for reflecting on what has been said. Each one can learn from the other; each person can become a mirror for the other.

Actually, in reflecting on the thought of the other by the way I react, by the way that I listen, by the way that I ask questions, by the way that I remain indifferent, I indicate what value I place on the words spoken to me. My attitude towards the other is a type of response which reveals to the other, in its own way, what I think of the value and quality of his words.

2. *The Second Element: The Teacher's Role*

Adolescents today are becoming more and more allergic to a teacher who is remote and abstract. Is it the result of a more democratic spirit? Is it because of their desire for more freedom? Is it due to their desire for dialogue in mutual respect and confidence? They want less a "father" than a "brother," less of a professorial style and more of a fraternal approach, less of an indoctrination and more of a witness. They want one who participates with them in the human struggle and one who himself is searching. They want a teacher who stimulates rather than commands.

This new emphasis requires two things:

1. The teacher must be part of the group; not over it, but inside, within the group.

2. The teacher must be for the service of the group so that the group will express itself and grow in freedom; and he must not try to direct the group to his own norms and objectives, even if they be apostolic objectives.

A teacher less directive, less of the master who rules—what does this mean?

Often enough, pedagogical tradition has considered the educator as a master who transmitted certain precepts and directions; he was one who instilled in his students a certain number of "good habits." The teacher was outside the group. He himself incarnated values and ideals. Having in his possession the keys of knowledge, he had to transmit a program. The successful absorption of the program was proven by an examination which qualified the student for a role in society. If a student passed a predetermined number of exercises and examinations, he and the teacher had both succeeded.

A. A TEACHER WHO IS PART OF THE GROUP

Adolescents today expect their teacher to be more democratic, in the sense that he participate with a certain type of equality in the group, in its researches, its struggles, its emotional life. They want someone who knows how they are thinking, who is attuned to their thought processes, and not someone who transmits knowledge which is apart from their time or basic inclinations. "Rather than be for or against a teacher, they want to bring him into their group, and they try to become attached to him in a personal way. If any teacher will not allow this, then he is classified as old-fashioned and out of date."[3]

B. A TEACHER WHO SERVES THE GROUP

Much more, adolescents expect their teacher not only to participate in the life of their group, but also to help the development of the group, to be of service to it. They want him to be less directive, less one who indoctrinates, but more one who stimulates, who awakens, who serves.

In a few words, one could say that the teacher of religion will not be considered so much the person who offers doctrine from behind a desk as the servant of the Christian group who helps them to ask the right questions, who helps them to express themselves, who helps them to listen to themselves. He is one who helps them to search for the truth, but one who does it with them. Finally, he is one who allows the group to give itself more deeply to the mystery of faith which they discover together. The role of the teacher is not to propose dogma as one who is not a part of the group, but, as someone who is in some true way a part of the group, slowly to go forward with his students towards the fullness of truth, starting from the individual insights and possibilities of each member of the group, and also starting from an active search into the living tradition of the Church.

3. A. Van Munster, in *Supplément de La Vie Spirituelle,* May, 1963.

3. AUTHORITY AND DIRECTION
IN GROUP EDUCATION

Have we considered the implications of the group approach and the less directive role for the teacher? Here are some: the necessity for an education of freedom and love so that faith may grow; the emphasis placed on dialogue and active research by members of the group rather than on the transmission of a monolithic program; a religious education structured less on a relation of student to teacher or to director, and more on the interpersonal communication of all the members of the group.

The new educational situation is that in which adolescents build up their own faith through sound group dialogue which is stimulated and deepened by the teacher. It is a situation in which each one is called on to discern and formulate his own group responsibilities, to play his own social role, and finally to discover and to fulfill his own profound vocation in the group, helped in all this by the teacher. Therefore, there is a corresponding new catechetical situation where authority is seen only in the service of the active search of the group.

But, one may object, in such an approach, what happens to the magisterial role, the more formal and directive approach in religious education? Moreover, is not the authority of revelation lessened or implicitly disparaged?

It is important to be well aware that the religion teacher is not a judge counting points in a debate; all through a class period he is effectively a teacher by the quality of the questions asked, by the deepening of the debates, if need be by the corrections, and

137

finally by the conclusion which takes in all the results of the class research and discussion, summarizing and clarifying the whole area of thought. It is true, however, that he does not teach as one who is above the group, an approach he may have used formerly. His authority in his new approach does not superimpose itself on the group from outside or above them; it is founded in the group, in the service of the group. Certainly, the teacher does not lose his essential role, a sacramental one, of the teaching Church; but he realizes it in another fashion: in stimulating discussion, in encouraging and guiding research, in supplementing and filling in on the material acquired by the students, and finally, and this is essential, in guaranteeing in the name of the Church the truth discovered by the group.

A type of non-directive approach which has been used frequently in Canada and France, often inspired by group-dynamics methods, has presented some problems. In particular, it has given rise to the following questions: Can there be in religious education an absence of direction to such an extent that the word of God is absent in some formal manner, and even held back?

The non-directive approach, it was learned, often plunges the group into a type of anguish or anxiety and internal confusion. Some theoreticians in group dynamics and psychoanalytical thought see in this reaction a necessary step for the growth of interior freedom in the group, that is, the death of the "father image," which removes the necessity of always reverting to authority. Another question which arises, then, is whether in the Christian education of adolescents, the absence of a helpful authority, which might create an anxiety situation, is something that is good and necessary. Is it necessary for adolescents to become free of the authority which the Father has in order to achieve freedom in faith?

These are delicate questions which cannot be quickly settled, and which, we believe, can only be answered in any definite way by discovering new forms of an authentic religious education through a dialogue between teachers and students.

1. Some Guides for Educational Rapport Between Teachers and Students

The teacher can fully adopt all that Carl Rogers means by non-directive if it is a question of human rapport, of attitudes of the heart, of the meeting of minds which establishes and sets up the climate for religious education between the teacher and students. Yet, is it not necessary to come to terms on what he means by these words?[4] We have noticed that many educators refer to Rogers to define for themselves a non-directive approach which tends more to the relationship between a psychoanalyst and his patient, or certain approaches in group dynamics which see anxiety as a value; and this precisely is the attitude that Rogers is combating: "What the therapist must free his client from is his anxiety." It is not a question, then, of creating an anxiety situation in the group by the absence of a teacher; "anxiety is an anti-therapeutic phenomenon." Rogers criticizes this too objective, too disinterested and external attitude of the psychoanalyst towards the client (considering it to be the chief fault of many of his "disciples"), and claims, on the contrary, the need for psychotherapy to have an attitude of empathy, of understanding, which

4. See in particular his *Counseling and Psychotherapy*.

seeks to create a climate of security and warmth. He dares to speak of a true love.

Rogers draws upon the thought of Martin Buber in order to define the human relation by an extremely human expression: to confirm the other (to strengthen the other). This seems to us the richest approach which has ever been formulated, not only to characterize the condition for a helpful relation, but more, to define the conditions for a positive and free relation with adolescents, by reason of our understanding of their psychological process during their stage of becoming, an age which needs confirmation and strengthening.

2. The Place of Non-Direction in Religious Education

Considering more precisely and carefully the idea of teaching and the question of the religious education of adolescents, it seems to us that it would be imprudent for a teacher to adopt the non-directive approach without qualification; rather, he must seriously reflect on it and adapt from it what is valid and useful in the context of his particular teenage group. In fact, the non-directive approach, if it is seen as "the absence of value judgment" or the lack of reference to established analyses of interpretation of situations or problems, leads finally to an absence of all reference to doctrinal content; and, by the same thinking, there would be an absence of teaching which would intrude in any way or go beyond in any fashion the immediate capabilities of the students.

How non-direction works in the field of psychotherapy is one problem; but how it applies in religious education or teaching in general is something else. To transfer the psycho-therapeutic

140

technique of non-direction to the field of teaching is, we strongly believe, a manifold error. In the first place, it violates the fundamental pedagogical rule that the objective truth, the doctrinal content, everything that is seen in relation to the learning student, must often precede or go before him, or even go beyond him, and at times be forced upon him. It is also an error in that we know, from the psychology of adolescence, that generally the student requires a more directive doctrinal approach in order to grow in freedom.[5] Too great an absence of direction in doctrine can throw him too forcefully into a sense of insecurity or in the direction of a life where the emphasis is on his own undirected and unguided desires for self-compensation rather than the opening of his spirit to an authentic freedom which can come from responsible maturity.

4. THE NECESSITY OF THIS APPROACH

1. Why the Group Structure?

The world of tomorrow demands. It demands men who will dialogue with one another, men alive to the social process and capable of working in it, men capable of a more authentic democratic approach to life.

5. With certain students, in particular with adolescents, it is possible that mental blocks may arise against religious education because of their over-exposure to religion, or because excessive authority was used on them in their religious upbringing. In such cases, perhaps a type of cure might occur through the use of the non-directive approach; but, of course, this cannot be made a general rule for the entire approach to the religious education of adolescents.

But in very many respects this future task of man is already a present concern, so much so that we who are teachers must prepare our students both for what already is and for what tomorrow will be. It is in our present age that the students find that they accomplish things in a new way, a way we call the group style, or better, the team approach.

The necessity for his approach, it would seem, is based not so much on the nature of things in today's world, but on our view of the history we are living. The team approach is an invitation to look closely at the signs of our time.

Gaston Berger has described the types of man we will have to educate for tomorrow. "We need for the future," he writes, "generous men open to exchanges with their fellow brothers, deeply sociable, not only in the superficial relations of everyday life, but in essential dialogue, as much as in team work, which more and more will mark professional, civic, and international life. They will have to rejoice spontaneously at successes around themselves, feel deep solidarity with one another, become joyously conscious of the 'birth of a planetary humanity,' which seems to be the greatest evolutionary fact of our times, but which also imposes on each person certain moral demands. For the dangers of destruction increase with the hope for growth and unity."[6]

How far we are from the non-involved middle-class man, or the individualistic concept of man!

In educating today's adolescents it is necessary to proceed from this new fact of life—the group or team.

This insistence on change in our educational attitude is not only motivated by the need to prepare for tomorrow, but it is also

6. Gaston Berger, *Prospectives,* October, 1961.

exacted of the teacher by his students. Of course, the group phenomenon, or sometimes the gang, does not always represent the ideal group we have been discussing, but it does constitute the basis, the foundation, from which we will have to proceed if we want our education to be true to life around us. While it is also true that in this country much has been done in terms of the educational team approach for students, this technique has not always been employed in the catechetical situation. Nor has there been much done in the way of writing which would provide religion teachers with the necessary preparation and guidelines for the successful implementation of this approach.

Although this new group existence is characterized by the fact of its members being together much of the time, one rarely sees all of the members of any one group meet in any organized way. Thus, "being together" means, in effect, reading the same magazines, listening to the same records, liking the same people, dressing in the same way, speaking the same language. The standards and principles of the group are assimilated by all its members; each tries to conform with the group ideals. When two or three members of the group happen to meet, they "shoot the breeze" about these magazines, records, people that they like; that's enough to be part of the crowd. They are happy because they have seen their friends. They've been out with the guys.[7]

Thus a new solidarity is being felt in which the factors of

7. We are conscious of the fact that this description does not apply to all adolescents today. In the first place, however, this is not so much a description of the 18 to 20-year-old group, but more of the rising generation of 14 to 17. In the second place, we are describing, more or less, lower to middle-class students, rather than high-upper-class students or students from very rural areas.

friendship and environment are diluted, almost disappearing, to be transformed into a new type of relationship in which comradeship has a greater part than friendship and in which doing things together and being together are more important than sharing plans, hopes, confidences.

Not that there are no more environmental and interpersonal friendships. On the one hand, however, adolescents do not want from friendship what they wanted in previous generations. Now relations tend to be more relaxed and less intimate, more simple and less exclusive. What really matters for teenagers now is to have the same insignia, the same status symbols or style of clothing, the same casualness in meeting, the same excitement about things going on, the same ease in personal relations which eliminates any thoughts about the future, the same feeling that each one can succeed. They are neither bitter nor enthusiastic, neither pessimistic nor optimistic; yet they cannot be called indifferent.

On the other hand, they take the world as it comes, as they find it. They have some hope, some love, some fear, some concern. With these and a place to hang their hat, they go on living. Because they are taken up by the crowd, they have little time to worry about their future, about making plans. Living here and now is enough for them. It can be said of them that they are better at creating a community than at realizing an ideal.

2. A Psycho-Sociological Analysis of Socio-Cultural Types

The community or crowd rather than a personal ideal, being together rather than seeking after one greater plan of life—this seems to characterize the new way of life.

In order to have a better insight into the possibilities and risks of this crowd concept, its values and its voids, and also to see it as part of a larger evolutionary picture, let us refer to the analysis and interpretations of David Riesman in his work *The Lonely Crowd*.[8]

Riesman distinguishes three socio-cultural types.

A. THE TRADITION-DIRECTED

This type, seen more in the small towns or the national ghettoes of large cities, is gradually disappearing in our society.

What counts for the young person of this type is to be molded in the ways and customs, the local traditions and sayings, the rules, the traditional forms. The guardians of the local culture, the influential elders of the town or community such as the priest, teachers, small business men, the mayor or the lawyer, set the way of life that must be followed unless one wants to be cut off from society. The law of growth in this type of society is the law of conforming to the pattern established by the elders of the community, of remaining faithful to the laws of the local culture. Here the key words and phrases are: rules, customs, the priest says, that won't do here.

B. THE INNER-DIRECTED

The second type could be largely found in the middle-class society and the Catholic schools to the beginning of this generation. Faced in our society with a wide diversion of cultural and per-

8. D. Riesman, N. Glazer, R. Denney, *The Lonely Crowd*, New Haven, 1953.

sonal choices, the parents and the schools took over the task of tradition (which the community could not) and molded the youth in long well-established lines of conduct, imposing on them a far-off ideal of another time and culture which they should spend their lives pursuing. This ideal was further exalted by teachers, spiritual directors, and even institutions.

These are the ones we have often called the elite, and who, in a pluralist society, incarnated the survival of the traditional ideals. Strongly inner-determined, a person of this type has a demanding super-ego; he is endowed with a sort of internal compass with the needle always pointed to the objective, the ideal he could wait for, "which permits him to direct himself in a predetermined manner to make the right choice in any new situation. He is always capable of maintaining a delicate balance between his own need for action in any area and the fluctuations of the world's thinking around him. He knows how to keep himself going and how to keep on balance, and, like a gyroscope, he can be directed from within, not requiring any directions from without."[9]

The key words and phrases here are: ideal, duty, personality, principles, leadership, a society where the father image dominates.

C. THE OTHER-DIRECTED

This type could be compared to radar because it is sensitive to all the currents, all the signals. It is appearing more and more today, especially in our suburban areas and middle-class city sections which have lost the sense of community tradition and where strong family ties are being weakened by reason of in-

9. J. Ledu, in *Catéchèse,* April, 1965.

creased family and personal mobility and changing social structures.

The other-directed type is the one that appeals to those adolescents whom we have described in terms of the new group or team approach to life. Left to themselves in a world where parental authority finds itself less and less effective and where teachers are often considered necessary perhaps but not relevant, these youths do not have any sound cultural models or guides whom they can follow at this time and whose values they can assimilate.

J. Ledu comments on Riesman's analysis: "The gyroscope type is threatened interiorly by a basic error, a distraction. It is not the ideal instrument; yet it is radar type now that is in prominence. The radar personality is like the antenna which is always turning in search of the signals which come to him from his contemporaries. This internal sensitivity to others develops in an extraordinary fashion, always conscious of the interests and behavior of others. This way of life is less established in terms of the principles of the family which are maintained within oneself; rather, it is more in terms of the approval or disapproval of the others. More concerned about keeping in with his equals, his peers, and anxious to pay any price to stay with the crowd, a person of this type will feel that he has arrived if he is capable of feeling at ease with everyone. It is less the fact of having a number of friends who share ideals, who keep us solidly on the ground; and more the idea of knowing yourself to be capable of having a wide circle of acquaintances, of being popular, of knowing people wherever you are."[10]

10. *Ibid.*

Van Munster has remarked on another characteristic of today's youth, "their vague restlessness, their vague uncertainty, which keeps them constantly on the move. They are not urged by a sense of duty but by their longing to be at home somewhere, by the feeling of uneasiness they get when they don't feel at home." What is important in their home life, therefore, is "the fact of being together: a quiet gathering around the television set, relaxing moments, everything blending together, everyone trying to make everyone else feel welcome, at home. . . ."[11]

The key words and phrases here are: success, the star, the guys, vacation, team, community, realism, group discussion, to each man a chance, and so forth; it is a society where the mother image dominates.

These classifications not only describe, but also reveal the psycho-sociological motivations of behavior. Educators are thus enabled to understand better through this detailed presentation how, except in some instances,[12] most adolescents are heading towards the other-directed grouping. In view of this an understanding of the approach to religious education through the group becomes more and more necessary.

From this lengthy analysis we can draw the following conclusion for our catechesis: What is essential for the group is that our aspects of teaching and information are never separated from an openness on our part which allows free and rich discussion. Doctrinal content and the valuable quality of dialogue are inseparable, to such an extent that often the group will only accept

11. A. Van Munster, *loc. cit.*
12. We are referring to those boarding schools where adolescents are still very much under parental authority and strong middle-class principles.

a doctrine when it is part and parcel of the group. Teaching as such has its peace and function only insofar as each member of the group feels that the subject under discussion comes alive in the group, so that there is a feeling of participation.

In this view, the educational content of a lesson tends to subordinate itself to the more important aspect of the group reaction and integration of the material that is presented for discussion. In this new situation, a different approach to teaching cannot be ignored. That is to say, the teaching we hope to propose to our students will be received less for its objective value than for its value as discussion material.

Thus, as Ledu suggests, "a presentation on the mystery of the Church, or any other topic for religious education, will remain foreign to the student if it doesn't reach him through the group, if the rich Christian sense of the lesson is not, at the same time, the means of bringing to each member of the group some value for the life he is living. For otherwise the educational aim and the purpose of the group are separated and we are beyond the conditions for a good program for religious education."[13]

Speaking in other terms, as long as the truth of faith does not become material for exchange, dialogue, discussion, something the students can put their teeth into, and also something that gives life and renews the group itself, the risk is great that the adolescents will not assimilate it and will not feel any concern over the matter.

We can mourn the passing of the days of the giants, men of ideals, the great and lonely leaders. But our time and, even more,

13. J. Ledu, *loc. cit.*

tomorrow demand another type of man. Are we going to ignore this sign of the time?

Still more, we believe that the coming of age of this new man, rooted in the social-community world, is an opportunity for the Church, for mankind itself. It is a chance for world unity and for the growth and the deepening of the person.

Do you really believe, some will say, that the emphasis on the group, vaguely defined and more often than not anonymous, having neither strong internal structure nor principles, is a sign of progress and development? Isn't the group more a sign of decline? The answer to these questions really depends on us, religious educators. It is certain that most groups, left to themselves, do not become human or Christian successes. What we have been trying to do is not defend any particular group approach; rather, we hope only to point out some of the many new possibilities for spiritual development that can be discovered in today's adolescents. Also, we cannot simply ignore the economic, social, and cultural forces of today which call urgently for a new type of educational approach and which require, therefore, a new type of educator.

Summarizing, we can say that our justification is less theological than prophetic. It is an invitation to read and to understand the signs of our time.

Now who can educate to a liberal, democratic, social consciousness better than a teacher whose personal and educational approach is that of the democratic and socially conscious type? Like father, like son, goes the saying. A man who lives by principles has a son tied to principles and progress; a teacher who guides, who is desirous of stimulating initiative and interpersonal relations, will have students with initiative and a consciousness of the other.

3. Why a Teacher Who Guides Rather than Governs?

What do we mean by a teacher who is more a friend and a brother? Again, it is the changes which have occurred in our society that here justify our response.

Based on highly structured levels of authority, individuals and communities in traditional society always looked to the next-higher authority in power. In such a society, individuals could reach higher social levels only by passing through all intermediate stages and only with the consent of the authorities at each level. Thus an individual might be under the authority of his own father in the family community, then that of a guild-master, the mayor of the town, the count, the bishop, and at the summit, the prince. Submission to these different authorities at any point was not only a virtue, it was a necessity. There was no other way to succeed.

In such a society, a young person's behavior was constantly regulated by reference to some authority and to well-established rules and customs. What one needed in order to enter adult life was the know-how, the customs, the good habits which made for good and loyal conduct. The key figure in such a situation was the father. The ideal educator was the one who transmitted principles and programs, who proposed to the young person a strong and well-structured personality with which he could identify.

Today's society, however, is very different. Individuals, because they are unceasingly called on to reinvent, to discover their own conduct and way of life and to further their knowledge, have very little use for one who merely tells him what to do, or for traditional approaches that no longer seem relevant. In our society the individual has the freedom to choose his own associates; he can select his own social organizations and groups; he can decide on his own sources of information and he feels free to adopt ideologies and religion which suit him. Modern society is structurally pluralistic, free, and democratic.

In such a context, why must there be this insistence on a teacher of the faith who is a guide, a friend, rather than a master? Because we are in the post-Christian era; we are no longer in a Christian society where the community itself supported the individual Christian. Adolescents today are exposed to all sorts of currents in the areas in which they live. How will they be able to believe if they cannot see the faith in a living witness? In a world where profane reality is too evident, how can we be content with a teaching that is lifeless, even if the material is technically correct and even adequately presented? The adolescent needs a teacher who is a witness, a person alive who announces the good news of life in himself, and who gives them the taste for the life that is full and rich, richer than the immediate life offered by the world today. He must be an absolutely trustworthy witness, a friend who opens the message by the very means of love.

In this difficult and impersonal world, who doesn't look first for a brother, rather than for a theorist who offers words without life, discourse instead of conversation? Like Thomas, the adolescent needs to feel with his own hands the resurrection; and today he can only experience the resurrection in a witness who is close to him. Outside of that, this present generation, nourished by science and facts, will only see in religious education words and a belief outside of reality. How much better if we, teachers, would learn to step down from our pedestals and be, before anything else, brothers who live and deepen our shared faith with our students.

5. SUGGESTIONS AND METHODS

1. *Creating Groups*

The teacher, at the beginning of the year, must feel responsible for forming those students who have come to him into a living group, and this can be especially difficult when the students come from markedly different backgrounds, or if, as it sometimes happens, many of the students have never (at least consciously) been in a group before. The teacher, then, before he begins his teaching, must first try to make himself part of the group.

In forming the group he should, first of all, create an atmosphere and a climate of dialogue, a climate based on mutual respect, on understanding, and on freedom in initiative. The teacher must help each individual discover his own value, what he can contribute to the group, and help him see himself in relation to others, and have each see that he has something to give. Without these preliminaries, which are indispensable, nothing can be done.

In the second place, the teacher will have to propose objectives which will bring the group together in common research: How can we work this together? Do you have any ideas? I might suggest . . . This might help . . .

153

2. *Developing in Students the Idea of Mutual Vocation*

Adolescents must become really convinced that group living, the team approach, helps them to be themselves and to discover other persons in a richer and better way. They must learn to think group or team and not only I; they must react to things with the group's concern in mind. It should not be "It displeases me," but "It's bad for the group."

Here are a few simple points:

—Teach the students to be in the service of the group, to find for themselves a very definite job for everyone's good, to be ready to have the group's interest go before their own.

—Teach them to feel responsible for the progress of the group. Bring them to be concerned about the group, to worry about its development and growth. For example, it is better to organize a class meeting to study the problems of the group rather than to keep complaining about them with one or two other people.

3. *Teaching Students to Work in and with the Group*

For students to be able to work effectively in teams, each must find his "place" in the group. Then they can be introduced to research, to development of ideas, to discussion. Whoever gets involved in a group situation will quickly learn what is expected of him: he offers himself and his availability. At the same time, he learns that the group approach offers certain riches, and also a certain solitariness. He learns to accept the constant tension between the fundamental solitude of the human condition in his own uniqueness and insights and the desire to communicate and share with the group. He at times feels alone because of his uniqueness and yet rich because of the times of sharing with others.

By way of example, here are five rules for group discussion or action:

1. Do not contradict a student, or discuss his opinion, until you have heard him out at length and then questioned him.

2. Stop yourself from speaking or asking questions when a student is speaking.

3. Before phrasing a question, ask yourself if it will interest the entire group. If the question interests only a very small minority, keep silent. If a student continually asks questions outside of the subject being discussed, the leader must either ignore the questions and give another student the right to speak, or at a later time take that student aside and privately discuss his questions with him.

4. Clearly think out your opinion before talking. It is forbidden to think aloud.

5. When the discussion rambles, or when it gets lost in abstractions, call in facts, examples.

Imagine that these rules, very simple in appearance, became part of the group process during a few months. If the teacher abided by them and the class picked up the spirit in them, what a change would take place in the group.

4. Introducing Students to Research

Adolescents must discover the Christian faith not only from the exterior teaching reproduced in texts, or from the teacher who stands before them, but also by active and personal searching and researching of the faith in all the human and Christian realities which surround him.

—Develop in students the habit of searching for documents and the art of knowing where to find them. Adolescents, when they become adults, should not have so much digested a program as developed a hunger for knowledge of God and acquired a method of discovering Him in a thousand realities and sources. They should have the know-how of interviewing people, the art of asking questions, of listening to others, of taking notes, and so forth.

—In religious education, we must be especially conscious of the need to develop in our students a hunger for the actual and living tradition of the Church, and a habit of referring to it. This supposes on the student's part both the desire for religious information and the capacity for seeing what is a simple opinion and what is a definition of faith, for understanding not only the historical words of a doctrine but also the deep meaning of a truth.

5. Giving Students a Sense of Mission

Can we be satisfied with forming a group in itself and for itself? It should be evident that we cannot.

It is important to educate groups not only for good interpersonal relationships, but also to develop relationships with the larger situations of the world. This is particularly the case today. We can no longer be content to form a group of Christians. This world, as it exists today, is markedly estranged from Christ and the Church. Our students mingle every day with non-Christians, with the indifferent, with non-believers. This situation is a fact of life, but it is also a providential call. Christians today are part of the world; instead of bemoaning this fact in a sterile fashion, why not look positively at the opportunities of evangelization which modern society offers?

It is also impossible to think of a religious education which develops in a "greenhouse" atmosphere. It is essential, on the contrary, that our students be educated in dialogue, in a language of evangelization which is notable for its timeliness and lack of archaisms and clichés. We must teach our groups to be open to other groups, to be able to dialogue with quality with all human beings, to be the way of transmitting the word of God to non-Christians.

How does a student discuss with his Protestant friends? How does he read his daily newspaper? How does he talk of friendship, religion, of the Church with his non-believing friends? Religious education must prepare him for these encounters, enable him to comprehend the language of others. If we do not so prepare him, we betray this sign of our time; we make a catechesis of the ghetto. One can even say that sooner or later a group not open to others will close in on itself. On the other hand, in educating to dialogue outside, we are opening to life and we are developing the group to its true finality.

6. REFLECTIONS

1. Does it appear in our own approach to the teaching of religion that we not only stimulate life in our student groups by our lessons and suggestions, but that, before anything else, we are also believers who are searching for the truth, who remain humbly

157

open to the needs of our students, our brothers in the faith? Are we a part of the group, or outside or above it?

2. Do we think of our teaching in terms of the life and spirit of the group, or are we more concerned with covering the material?

3. Are we sufficiently concerned about the group as a group, so as to focus the attention of the group on a particular question, to have the group come together in the search for truth? Do we address ourselves to individuals, or do we speak to persons who are joined together in the same search?

4. In the plans for action which we suggest, are we conscious enough of stressing the necessity for group action? Are we concerned to have everyone involved in one or another activity, helping each one to find his role, or are we content to call on the more reliable and stronger personalities in the group?

VII.

THE WORLD VIEW

Religious education will transmit the message of Christ nourished by the human and religious values of all men. It will educate the group to express and to develop its faith in the widest catholic dialogue, open to the whole world.

1. THE MEANING OF THIS APPROACH

This approach, in certain respects, is an enlargement and a further development of the basic group approach. It is no longer sufficient to teach a man only in relation to his immediate contacts or group, his own city or town, or even his own country. An educational formation that is limited to one's own culture or nation is unthinkable in the second half of the twentieth century. In the spirit of our time, education must open a student to the whole world.[1]

1. *We must transmit the faith today in a broader perspective, and with a more universal Christian and cultural outlook, and*

1. We should note that the way to the universal is through the singular; the opening to the universal, however, does not deny the function of the singular, of the one culture. Otherwise, there would be a universal being and a type of citizen of the world without root, without background, less than a complete human being.

remove the too narrowly limited and nationalistic trappings that surround our religious training.

God is not restricted to one people, one culture, one place. To know God truly as the Lord of the universe requires that we make an effort to release Him from one culture, one country, and that we present Him to the world as a God of many different human faces, a God who is Chinese as well as American, a God of all classes, of the free and the oppressed. He is the God of man.

2. *We must see to it that the adolescent learns to nourish his faith by dialogue, by open and fruitful discussion with those outside his limited world.*

It is not sufficient that our students learn the faith only from their immediate surroundings and contacts and through the program and approach of their teacher. They need other sources that are wider ranging and more universal. The teacher must be aware of this need and consider its possibilities and potential. He must see to it that his students' faith unfolds and develops by contacts and dialogue with those who are different and foreign to them.

It would be of great purpose, therefore, to have our students come into lively contact with people from areas other than their own city or from other parts of the country, or from other churches. This exposure will enrich our students with the ideas of universality and would enable those who are their Christian brothers especially to share their values with them. Our students would be able to adopt an attitude of positive openness to the values which are also in non-Christian religions. Finally, it would establish an active and sympathetic communication with all the values inherent in civil society, in the non-religious world.

160

To describe this section of our teaching we can provide our students with an image, a sign. And it is that of Pope Paul VI leaving the walls of the Vatican City for Jerusalem, Bombay, the United Nations headquarters in New York, going to countries having different cultures and different approaches to life, becoming a citizen of the world and a pilgrim throughout the universe. He did not go as a head of state, but as a brother of man, seeing Christ in all his brothers and announcing Him in the language and tradition of each society.[2]

2. THE NECESSITY AND IMPORTANCE OF THE WORLD VIEW

Why this new emphasis on the universal?

At first sight, such an approach might very well appear to be futuristic for its own sake; yet this is not actually the case. For a world outlook is what the time demands, and not only demands but has been prepared for, and must prepare for. Where once the world consisted of nations having little relation with or interest in one another, and in many cases not even being aware of the existence of other nations, it is now the case that the world has become a group of nations. The world is a union of nations, sharing common economic needs, sharing their cultural and technological genius with one another, sharing the same religious faiths, differing in or sharing political structures as the case may

2. In Jerusalem, Paul VI used the greetings of the Near East; in Bombay he admired and used in his talks the wisdom of the Hindus; at the United Nations he spoke as an "expert on humanity." It was in the new style inaugurated by John XXIII, who said, "The whole world is my family."

be, all faced with the same bigotry, the same poverty. For all these reasons—economics, political, cultural—internationalism is an irreversible trend. The barriers between nations are gradually falling down, and taking their place are ties which unite them.

The man of today, therefore, if he is to be a viable part of his world, is obliged to do away with any aspiration to self-sufficiency; if he hopes to help change this changing world for the better, he can only do so with the help of others. And if this is the case, then he must know who the others are.

Although the adolescent in America does not as a rule travel to foreign lands, he is nevertheless able to expand his view of the world by taking advantage of the international media which are at his disposal—notably television, and to some extent films. Telstar coverage of world events, video tapes reporting on other countries, news of student political action in foreign lands, —all of these show him a way of life which is different from his own. He can no longer think of his own way of life, his own culture, his own nation, as the only way. For these influences from other lands are living ones.

Thus it is that the growing international exchanges on all levels will more and more shape the world of tomorrow and force men to live on a world-wide basis. A corresponding new type of human personality is therefore appearing, characterized by a communication with and open-mindedness to all the dimensions of man, and of nations.

Is it more honest to say, however, that this internationalizing process now going on is more the concern and interest of the adult? It would seem that the student is far removed from world problems since he is too much involved in his family, social, and

162

school life. Moreover, is it even suitable and possible for him to have a wider view of his country and of the world at this stage of his life? We think it is suitable, and that in fact students today are very much involved in what is going on in their country and in the world. Students today may still read the sports page of their newspaper first, but it is no longer the case that that is all they read. Student political rallies and student participation in the civil-rights movement are convincing signs that students not only are, but very much want to be, involved in national and international life.

Some of the reasons why the adolescent national and world views have been expanded in recent years are:

—war and peace are being seen as global concepts;

—war and rumblings of war in distant lands have made youth conscious of a world outside their own limited lives;

—the visit of Pope Paul VI to the United Nations showed an open acceptance of a Christian leader of the international view of man;

—the Peace Corps and VISTA offer opportunities to American youth to share themselves with others in different parts of their country and in distant lands and cultures;

—travel outside America is becoming more accessible and cheaper;

—students are aware of space, of almost no limits to man's explorations;

—the civil-rights movement has made many adolescents extremely alive to the needs of others;

—entertainers from outside America, European customs and fads, all exercise a shaping influence.

163

Recently, some students from a school in upper New York state visited a slum section in Harlem and on another trip toured the United Nations building. In both cases there was a sense of genuine wonderment over the contact with a different world, but what was more significant was that the students learned to see, accept, and admire values different from their own, to find truth in other cultures and backgrounds and in economic, political, and social structures different from their own. This limited contact made these suburban middle-class students alive to man in a concrete and more universal fashion than they had ever been able to experience in words alone.

Sociologist Y. M. Cloitre, in an interview on youth and its idols, remarked, "I see in this youth . . . a certain universalism which goes beyond social and racial barriers, a real freedom of judgment unhampered by the bonds of conformity, the need for wide friendships (yet too frequently limited to more immediate contacts), respect for religious beliefs and opinions of others . . ."[3]

This new situation, this change of spirit, must be seized by us not only as an indisputable fact which demands some adaptation in our teaching attitudes, but also as a privileged situation, a providential moment, as a point in time beneficial to the Church and to our students.

1. An Opportunity for the Church

This historical situation represents an unprecedented opportunity for the Church. Never before has the Holy Spirit so urged the Church to become more universal, more catholic. The necessity

3. *Hello,* November 15, 1964.

for international existence which is being felt in all lands is also urging the Church to deepen its sense of universality, to discover its own spiritual dimension in a wider and richer perspective. The idea of a Christian who is universal in relation to man is essentially based on the mystery of man enriched by Christ, who brought life to man's relationships, who gave it a dimension beyond man's own self, who by His resurrection gave men a life which opened them to all others.

Thus our concern today in making our encounters with others more meaningful and in entering more fully into the mystery of human encounter by a more universal view of man, also helps us to understand more profoundly the height, the depth, the richness of the mystery of the Risen Christ. The more intensively and extensively we meet man in his many faces, the more completely we will meet Christ in whom all men share life. To discover the universality of the Church is not only to know all truth in and from it; more, it is to know the Church as that community through which truth can and must be proposed so that it can bring men together.[4]

2. An Opportunity for Adolescents

The opportunity for the Church to become more youthful and more international in this new world, to become more internationally catholic, also concerns the Christian life of the adolescent.

Students now have an opportunity to be more open to the

4. "[The Church] offers her services to all peoples by way of promoting the full development of the human person, for the welfare of earthly society and the building of a world fashioned more humanly." *Declaration on Christian Education,* Article 3.

beatitudes and to the Spirit of the kingdom of God. Nothing better prepares a student for the surprising meaning of the kingdom of God than to be shaken out of his own comfortable culture and to be exposed to another's way of life. He is then no longer self-contained in his own world, unwilling to change or open. Nothing can help him see his own limitations and inadequacies better than to be in dialogue with another and then to see himself and others in a new relation. He is no longer the only ideal. When he welcomes humbly other cultures, other races, he begins to make ready for God's kingdom. The poverty of heart which every authentic interpersonal meeting requires is the best disposition for his meeting of the Lord, this stranger who is his brother.

Adolescents now have a chance for a renewal and a growth of charity. World hunger, the underdeveloped and underprivileged nations, the Peace Corps, all are appeals addressed to youth. We have seen how quickly adolescents respond to these calls as soon as they hear them.[5] Is not this appeal, in our time, a permanent source for a renewal and growth in love? Nothing teaches charity faster than being told of another who is in need.

There is now a chance for the adolescent to purify his faith and also to extend his faith in wider horizons. Meeting our brothers of the whole world is discovering in a certain way the

5. We are thinking here of the many possibilities for service and international exchange, possibilities we should enlarge upon while at the same time being conscious of the dangers for the adolescent. From one point of view, we can consider the emerging nations and underdeveloped areas of this country as rendering us a great service. Before we think of what we do and can give them, we should think of how they give to us in allowing us to help them. What greater service can a person give to another than to make the other feel useful, necessary; when he offers the other a field of operation where he can express himself and discover in himself a new value which makes him richer?

infinite variety of the face of God. It is to become painfully aware
of what we mean by the breadth and depth of the Spirit of God,
the infinite dimensions of His love and mercy. It is in the measure
that we believe in true exchange, true openness to others, that
men, that we Christians enter most fully into the catholicity of
the faith, finding again each time the totality of man and the full
dimensions of Christ.

3. THE DANGERS OF THE WORLD VIEW

First of all, it is important to be very conscious of the fact that
the opportunity for broader national and international exchange
is also a great danger. The young Christian does not always realize, especially as a member of a group, that he, or the group, is
not the center of the world. He then discovers that others are
living in truth, and that sometimes these others have even a
greater sense of values than he has. He may then ask himself, at
a time when he is not fully prepared to find an answer: What
good is my faith?[6]

Precisely, it is not necessary that an adolescent lose his faith
or fall into relativism. We know that certain false or insufficient
attitudes await him: indifferentism, syncretic or integrist views.

In the present crisis of theological demythologization and de-
dogmatizing, a healthy attitude towards the universal can represent the best approach in education. Nothing is more apt to give

6. And the problem here is all the more serious when the faith has
been absolutely bound to forms which have hardened or on which have
been conferred a sort of immutability that is untrue: the way to say Mass,
the way to express dogma, and so forth. How did these forms of faith
and the religious life become fossilized, unless it was by a monolithic and
authoritarian teaching, by restricting form and language to one country,
one culture, one approach only?

balance to faith and also to purify it of unnecessary accretions than a better knowledge of the totality of man, of man's values and expressions. For, "if there is a God," one can only discover Him in the totality of man. That religion is true which joins in the most complete way all that is in man and which gives man his most perfect meaning and fullness. And whoever goes on a pilgrimage to meet universal man also takes a step in meeting God.

There is no doubt that such a pilgrimage requires prudence, the very same prudence of the Church. The Church demands that we stress at all times in our teaching the sense and values of its teaching, the value and the limits of its symbols and formulas, and finally the need for all of the faithful to join in the same pilgrimage of the Church towards the final kingdom.

In the measure that the faith has already been expressed and understood in a manner truly catholic and international, freed from an exclusively western outlook, then we can prepare our students to meet the challenges that travel and exchange will bring to them and their thinking on the faith. Without this preparation, our students may one day find themselves in a very small world, in a world where it is easy and convenient and perhaps inevitable not to have any faith at all.

4. SUGGESTIONS

Trips to foreign lands; an understanding of America itself with its different classes, cultures, approaches, personal contacts with European, South American, Asian, and African students; an introduction to and exploration of world literature, —all these and more are part of the growth that must come from an adolescent so that his small world will be increased in size and meaning before he enters early adulthood. The sensitive period of adolescence cannot be passed by for a later time. Later is often too late. People can become prisoners of the structures and organizations to which they have committed themselves. They become unconsciously bound to the same routine and thought processes and sometimes become incapable of the spirit of listening to others and of accepting differences of opinion. They become, in effect, open only to themselves and closed to the world.

Therefore, here are some suggested approaches on how the teacher can help open his students to the world.

1. The Attitude of the Teacher

The broad personal and international view, as we have said, is first of all proper to adults, and it is through the teacher's views and actions that his students will come to live themselves in a spirit of universal dialogue. If the teacher has not put all the force of his prestige and his friendship into helping his students understand (even though they are still somewhat self-centered) the importance of other peoples, cultures, beliefs, then how can they proceed to the new world where the emphasis is on dialogue and universal understanding?

What do students today expect from a teacher? Less than ever a spirit of propaganda, or a doctrinaire or ideological approach. What they essentially need in a teacher is a respect for the other, for what the other can be. What is important is the acceptance of the other, the spontaneous taste for discussion and dialogue and a desire to know everything. In brief, what is involved here is a certain manner of being at ease in the world, not being naïve certainly, but also not being too confused about it. It is the wide-open and sympathetic look at the world and at man and what man will be. It is being present to the whole world as Christ is present, in a spirit of covenant. In this manner we can contribute to the education in faith of our students.

Such a spirit also supposes a certain approach in planning, organizing time, finances, and work. The teacher must know what is going on around him in his country, in the world, even if only by reading magazines and newspapers and books. He must not only know the actual situations, the facts of a situation, but also the currents of thought and the organizations and movements that work for man's progress and growth and for unity on a world-wide level: the progress of emerging nations, the work of UNESCO, the non-violence movement. Is it not also worth-while for us as teachers to commit ourselves to one or more international or national movement which appeals to our own personal need for action and for information?

2. Inter-City and International Student Dialogue

It is important, in this age of travel, to encourage Christians from other areas to express their faith and to play a providential role in our own classes of religious education, for they can widen our horizons and can make us reflect on the universality of the Church and our own limitations. Especially in some university centers, there are thousands of students from other countries working on the graduate and undergraduate levels. There are also many visiting professors. Have we missed this opportunity? Are we aware that we can help these people from other lands enrich themselves by giving something of themselves to us? We ourselves will be enriched by opening to these other people.

Some concrete suggestions:

1. Invite a Christian from another country who is studying or working nearby to express his idea of faith before your students.

2. Make your students aware of the presence of foreign students in the area, of the clubs and associations of these students.

3. Invite students from other socio-economic, racial, or religious backgrounds to your classroom for a discussion. Preferably, a social gathering should follow this meeting.

In other words, we must discover the Spirit active in the world in all human realities and searchings.[7] We must develop the capacity of enriching the faith through many exchanges and not only through the lessons given by the teacher in religious instruction.

We can use all the resources, religious or secular, in our teaching of religious education with an international and universal view. They may be newspaper or magazine articles, photographs, guest speakers, interviews, anything which helps the student see how other people, how other religions, understand life.

Here are some key ideas for a possible lesson on freedom which opens the students to a more universal view.

7. "The Catholic Church rejects nothing which is true and holy in these [non-Christian] religions. She looks with sincere respect upon those ways of conduct and of life, those rules and teaching which, though differing in many particulars from what she holds and sets forth, nevertheless often reflect a ray of that Truth which enlightens all men." *Declaration on the Relationship of the Church to Non-Christian Religion,* Article 2.

One approach:

—what does freedom mean to someone who is crippled or handicapped?

—what does freedom mean to a Negro?

—what does freedom mean to an Eastern European?

—what is freedom in an emerging African nation?

—what is freedom to a factory worker?

Second approach:

—the desire of an adolescent for freedom;

—the search of all men for freedom;

—freedom, the desire of man through all ages;

—freedom, a gift of God;

—freedom of the sons of God.

4. REFLECTIONS

1. Is it clear to our students that we are searching for the many images of God through the many images of man?

Have we shown how revelation can be found in the values of all men?

2. Have our students become aware of the fact that the Church is not only American or Western European, but that it is truly universal? Also, have we given them the message of God through our personal witness, and through those experiences and cultural insights which come to us from all our Christian brothers throughout our country and the world?

3. Have we tried seriously to establish contact and a meaningful dialogue with people outside our limited world, either with

people from a different cultural and social level in our country, or with people from other lands?

4. Have our discoveries of other ways of life, of different ideas —in short, of the world—changed our approach to teaching? Are we in some measure confident that our students, when they leave our classroom, will live in a larger world than the one they came from?